ADVANCE PRAISE

"An entertaining and authentic collection of highly engaging anecdotes, hard-won life lessons, and unbelievable stories generously shared by experienced Silicon Valley CEO Mike Grossman for the benefit of future leaders. This book imparts wisdom with a humility and reflectiveness that is refreshing, and a sense of humor and candor that makes each message immediately accessible. An easy and enjoyable read with worthwhile and valuable learnings."

—KELLY BAYER ROSMARIN, CEO and Group Managing Director, Australian Unity; Former CEO, Optus

"Mike Grossman has written an unconventional and deeply human book that highlights the messy, unpredictable nature of running a company. His honest reflections on luck, timing, and failure are delivered through a series of personal stories that are as thought-provoking as they are entertaining. If you're looking for a realistic portrayal of the entrepreneurial journey, this is it."

—KEWSONG LEE, Founder and CEO, BellTower Partners; Former CEO, The Carlyle Group

"The format is great and the storytelling is terrific. A young executive in either a small or large enterprise could save themselves many years of agony if they read this book and take it to heart. But alas, that's not how the system works. We go to graduate school, then work in consulting or investment banking and then perhaps try to start something. With a little luck and good timing some find success and then they write books about how smart or clever they were and how they had it all figured out from the start! *Failure Is an Option* is a breath of fresh air."

—CARLOS RODRIGUEZ, Former CEO and Executive Chair, ADP

"Leadership is not about avoiding failure; it's about navigating it with humility, integrity, and resilience. *Failure Is an Option* strips away the mythology of Silicon Valley and replaces it with something far more valuable: truth. Mike Grossman writes with uncommon honesty about the emotional and ethical realities of leadership. I found this book both grounding and generous, a gift to anyone willing to lead when outcomes are uncertain."

—BRAD SMITH, President, Marshall University; Former Chairman and CEO, Intuit

"*Failure Is an Option* is a refreshing and deeply human look at the courage it takes to lead with heart. It beautifully captures the empathy needed to navigate the startup roller coaster while never losing sight of the people who make the journey possible."

–AMY ERRETT, Founder and CEO, Madison Reed; Former General Partner, Maveron Ventures

"Mike Grossman's new book, *Failure Is an Option*, not only reveals the truth about entrepreneurship's probability of failure but also shares what to do about it. Leadership books, especially autobiographical ones, rarely discuss setbacks in our success-oriented culture of self-help press, going back to Benjamin Franklin, Norman Vincent Peale, Dale Carnegie, and Stephen Covey. Grossman constructively challenges the fantasy of an endless success spiral. Studies of folk heroes across cultures, centuries, and continents demonstrate that failure is not only an option but a necessary stage of punctuating the career trajectory of heroic character. Grossman was never bitter from setbacks. Only a few make it through the cauldron of defeat, but those who are resilient from derailments are better, stronger, and heroic."

–JEFFREY SONNENFELD, Lester Crown Professor of Management Practice, Yale; Founder, Yale Chief Executive Leadership Institute; Author of *Firing Back*

"As a former operating executive and now a corporate director, I read a lot of business books. *Failure Is an Option* is different. It's a refreshingly honest look at what it actually takes to launch and run a VC-backed startup. Having led six such companies – some successful, some not – author Mike Grossman offers his lessons learned through a series of pithy, candid, and relevant stories – easy to read and hard to forget. This isn't a glossy success story nor a how-to manual. It's a candid account of missed calls, hard trade-offs, and good and bad luck that come with building something new. For entrepreneurs, operators, investors, and anyone curious about life inside a startup, *Failure Is an Option* pulls back the curtain and takes you inside a Silicon Valley CEO's head and heart. It's a book you'll want on your desk whether you're considering an entrepreneurial journey or are far down that path."

–CHRISTIANA SMITH SHI, Founder, Lovejoy Advisors; Co-Author of *Career Forward;* Former President of Direct-to-Consumer, Nike; Former Senior Partner, McKinsey & Company

"Mike Grossman doesn't just share the victories (though he's had his share). He walks you through the missteps, the bad luck, and the decision-making amidst uncertainty that define startup leadership. It's candid, insightful, and quietly reassuring for anyone who's in the arena and looking around to see if they're doing it correctly."

–GREG SANDS, Founder and Managing Partner, Costanoa Ventures

FAILURE IS AN OPTION

FAILURE IS AN OPTION

REFLECTIONS OF A SILICON VALLEY CEO

MIKE GROSSMAN

WASHINGTON, DC

Ideapress Publishing | www.ideapresspublishing.com

Cover Design: Ploy Siripant
Interior Design: Jessica Angerstein
Cataloging-in-Publication Data is on file with the Library of Congress.

Hardcover ISBN: 978-1-64687-246-6

Special Sales
Ideapress books are available at a special discount for bulk purchases for sales promotions and premiums, or for use in corporate training programs. Special editions, including personalized covers, a custom foreword, corporate imprints, and bonus content, are also available.

1 2 3 4 5 6 7 8 9 10

To Wati

Every morning when I wake up,
I think about the same two things:
how I need to make the day count,
and how grateful I am that you walked into my life.

CONTENTS

INTRODUCTION

Several years after my wife and I got married, I decided to write a holiday letter that would be sent to friends and family. The letter was fairly typical – which is to say, not very interesting – and summarized what we had done the previous 12 months. The following year, I wrote a similar letter. The third year, however, I decided to branch out.

I thought, wouldn't it be more compelling, both for me and the people reading the letter, if I took a more innovative approach? And gradually, an idea began to take shape.

The concept was to treat each year's letter as a creative writing exercise, but with specific rules of engagement. First, each letter needed to tell that year's story in a distinct and surprising way. I would never repeat myself with respect to voice, style, mood, narrative structure, or characterization; each year's letter needed to be different from every letter I had previously written. Second, I would never again write a holiday letter that was, in any way, conventional. The creative twist would vary from year to year, but there would always be a twist. Perhaps I would focus on one person in the family, or one specific experience. Perhaps time wouldn't be linear. Perhaps the language I used would be symbolic or allegorical. Perhaps the point of the letter wouldn't be revealed until the end. What I hoped was that people would read each year's installment and think – what an interesting, unusual letter; it's so different from any holiday letter that I've ever read before.

In a broader sense, I decided to metaphorically think of each year's letter as a patch in a patchwork quilt. The "quilt" was a "book" that I was writing in slow motion, one short chapter a year, that, in the aggregate, would tell the story of our lives.

I ended up writing holiday letters for 25 consecutive years. It was a good run, until I ran out of ideas. I eventually got to the point where I couldn't figure out how to continue making each of the letters distinct. So I stopped.

Over the next decade, I wrote a lot – thousands of emails, texts, Slack messages, etc. – but nothing creative. Then, I decided to write this book.

My motivation was clear. Although many books have been written about Silicon Valley, few focus on the real-life experience of running an early-stage, venture-funded technology company. And since I've run six of them, I have a unique perspective. Sharing that perspective seemed worthwhile.

What was less clear was how to best tell the story. I hoped to share lessons based on my personal experiences, but I had no interest in writing a traditional business memoir. Nor did I have any interest in writing a traditional "how-to." The one thing I (emphatically) knew was that if I was going to write a book, it needed to be original and unconventional.

And then inspiration struck. I may not have written a book before in any traditional sense, but I had many years of experience in writing holiday letters. So that, in effect, is what I decided to do.

Failure Is an Option is the result, a collection of 44 "holiday letters" – well, short stories. Each is autobiographical, concise, highlights a specific lesson or theme, and, with a couple of exceptions, stands on its own, complete and self-contained. In a sense, they can be read in any order, and purposely so.

I also followed several other rules of engagement. I intentionally didn't put the stories (or chapters) in chronological order. I also intentionally excluded most dates. In my view, the timeline simply doesn't matter. If someone wants to know more about the sequence of events and rough chronology, they can always check my LinkedIn profile.

Moreover, I generally avoided providing details about my operational playbook. I'm interested in examining the key issues faced by Silicon Valley CEOs and their practical, ethical, and emotional implications. I'm much less interested in offering tactical, prescriptive, one-size-fits-all solutions.

For the people who read this book, I have three main goals in mind. First, I hope you find it thought-provoking and entertaining. Second, I hope it provides you with a better sense of what running an entrepreneurial technology company actually *feels* like. And third, I hope you conclude that it's unlike any business book you've ever read before.

THE REAL SILICON VALLEY

Hear the words *Silicon Valley*, and what comes to mind? For most people, I think the answer is either billionaires like Elon Musk, Mark Zuckerberg, and Steve Jobs, or the transformative companies they founded (Tesla, Meta, Apple). In other words, when people think of Silicon Valley, they think of the entrepreneurs and organizations that have achieved the greatest financial success.

That's understandable. I would probably have a similar perspective had I chosen a different career path. But the truth is that the Musks, Zuckerbergs, Teslas, and Metas of the world are an aberration. In many ways, they aren't the real Silicon Valley. They're the exception rather than the rule.

The real Silicon Valley is more about failure than success. Fewer than 1 percent of startups succeed in raising venture capital,[1] and of the ones that do, only 25 percent end up with a positive return on investment (ROI).[2,3] Moreover, most of the 25 percent are only moderately rather than massively successful.

Even companies that ultimately have a great financial outcome face enormous adversity along the way. They often fail, or at least struggle, for many years before meaningful progress is made. And even when meaningful progress is made, something typically goes wrong, and progress comes to a grinding halt.

> **It's not for the faint of heart. Running a company in Silicon Valley is an enervating, emotionally draining, gut-wrenching experience.**

It's a psychological roller coaster that goes down more than up – a metaphorical Omaha Beach on D-Day – a relentless exercise in self-delusion and masochism.

I've spent 30 years running companies in Silicon Valley, and it's been a wild ride. My stats speak for themselves. I've been the CEO of six early-stage, venture-funded companies. These companies have collectively pursued 18 different business models, 12 of which ended up failing. Five of the six companies required layoffs. Two had multiple rounds of layoffs. Only three of the six ever exceeded $10 million in annual revenue. Only one exceeded $50 million in annual revenue.

Through the decades, I've received funding from 12 venture capital firms, three public corporations, one hedge fund, and dozens of angel investors. All six of the companies were ultimately acquired. The largest deal was for $400 million. The smallest was a $250,000 fire sale.

Some of the companies were severely disrupted by macroeconomic adversity. One was on the verge of doing an IPO when COVID-19 suddenly emerged. Another was on the verge of being acquired by Mastercard when the Great Recession suddenly emerged. And this latter company was disrupted again three years later, when Congress passed a law that effectively destroyed the company's business model.

At one point or another, all six companies faced an existential crisis. Three were persistently in a state of existential crisis. Describing all of this as a wild ride may be an understatement.

Do I have any regrets? Of course, the list is long. When you're a Silicon Valley CEO, you constantly have to make decisions based on limited information, and the inevitable consequence is that you make a lot of mistakes.

And some of these mistakes end up being highly significant. Sometimes the mistakes relate to strategy. Sometimes they relate to execution. Often they relate to people. It's baked into the cake and is unavoidable.

Nonetheless, while I regret many individual decisions I've made, I don't regret the choice of career. It hasn't been easy, but it has always been interesting. It hasn't always been fun, but it has always been challenging. And I've learned an enormous amount along the way – about entrepreneurship, leadership, and myself. This book is an attempt to share some of those insights.

UNLEARNING THE WRONG LESSONS

Sometimes we learn the wrong lessons. One of the fundamental lessons I learned as a kid was that there is a direct correlation between effort and results. At school, when I studied harder, I got better grades. The more I practiced activities like tennis, baseball, and piano, the better I played. So I initially assumed that the same rule would apply to entrepreneurship and being a CEO. The more I worked, the more successful the business would become. It seemed to be a truism. And that perspective gave me the confidence necessary to quit my job and co-found a company when my wife was nine months pregnant. Because I knew in my gut that success was inevitable. All I had to do was apply myself with sufficient diligence and relentlessness.

I wasn't entirely naive. I didn't expect success to be immediate. I realized it would require a lot of effort and grit. But I implicitly assumed that, in the end, effort and grit would be sufficient.

Of course, if you had spoken to me at the time, I would have professed humility. I would have acknowledged that leaving my job to start a company was highly risky and uncertain. But I didn't really mean it. My humility was merely performative. The truth was that I was certain I would succeed because I had always succeeded before.

Unfortunately, I had learned the wrong lesson. I had assumed that my experience, first as a student and then later as an employee, would directly apply. In reality, however, neither experience was especially relevant. That's not to say that grit and effort don't matter as a Silicon Valley CEO. They matter a great deal and are prerequisites to success. But they're hardly sufficient.

What I failed to perceive was the difference in context. In an academic setting, students have considerable control over the outcome. The educational system is designed to reward hard work. Of course, some students are more capable than others, and that plays a role in their results. But success in the form of good grades is generally achievable if enough effort is applied.

The dynamics are similar, or at least somewhat similar, in most professional environments. While employees often have limited authority, they can usually influence their personal success. The harder they work, the more likely their performance will be well regarded. It doesn't always work out that way, but the odds are good.

> **As a CEO, however, success isn't defined by personal performance. Success depends instead on how well the company performs, and how hard you work isn't the determining factor. A wide range of factors affect company performance, and as a CEO, you have a lot of influence over some, a little influence over others, and no influence over many.**

When I realized the truth, it was a humbling and startling revelation. It meant that I could do everything in my power in terms of effort, grit, focus, discipline, and perseverance – and fail. I could do an outstanding job individually and fail. I could hire an amazing group of people, all of whom do outstanding work, and fail. I could collaborate with those amazing people to build an innovative, exciting product that solves important problems and delights the customers who use it, and fail.

I first became a CEO in 1996 after co-founding a fintech company named LiveCapital. It was a year after Ron Howard's *Apollo 13* was released, a film that featured many memorable lines, including the classic "Failure is not an option."[4] In the early days of LiveCapital, my close friend and co-founder, Scott Belser, and I effectively adopted this line as our mantra. Whenever any challenge arose, we would remind each other that failure was not an option. As time progressed, however, our perspective shifted. We came to understand that "Failure was most definitely an option." And, on our darkest days, when gallows humor became one of our most important coping mechanisms, we would plaintively lament that "Success is not an option."

TIMING IS EVERYTHING

When I embarked on my journey as a Silicon Valley CEO, I believed that building a successful company was largely within my control. I had what I would describe as a "business school perspective" about what was most important. If asked to provide a list of key success factors, I would have talked about things like focusing on a large market, identifying an unmet customer need, hiring a talented team, building a great solution, raising sufficient funds, doing extensive research and rapid experimentation, setting clear objectives, defining a viable business model, and working exceptionally hard. To a great extent, I would have been right. All of these items really are critically important. But it would never have occurred to me to include timing on the list. And one of the main things I've learned is that timing is everything.

Let me share a story from my experience at LiveCapital that brings this to life. The company was founded during the early days of the internet. Our concept was provocative: make it possible for a small business to apply for a loan in five minutes and get approved in real time by multiple banks. It was a bold and exciting idea with the potential to revolutionize small business lending. Once we realized the opportunity existed, we dove in headfirst.

The next several years were a blur. We raised more than $50 million from prominent investors, including Kleiner Perkins and Bill Ackman; expanded our team from 3 to 125 people; built and launched the world's first online marketplace for small business lending; signed deals with more than 50 leading financial institutions, including American Express, Citibank, and Wells Fargo; and generated a significant amount of publicity.

We were hot. From a customer standpoint, we were receiving more small business loan applications than any bank in the world, and the volume kept steadily increasing. And, on a personal level, people were constantly seeking me out: job candidates looking to be hired, reporters in search of a scoop, venture capitalists (VCs) hoping to invest, and investment bankers eager to take us public. Most memorably, in September 2000, my wife, four-year-old son, and I had the chance to attend the Sydney Olympics as guests of investment banking firm Salomon Smith Barney. We were treated to a beautiful suite at the Ritz-Carlton, box seats for the opening ceremony, and tickets to the men's gymnastics competition. Only two other people were guests of Salomon Smith Barney that weekend: a young, seemingly introverted entrepreneur I had never heard of named Elon Musk and his new wife, Justine.

All told, it was an incredible experience. The company and I were on a rocket ride to the stars, and success seemed inevitable.

But there was a problem – a problem of epic proportions. The business model wasn't working. To generate revenue, we needed loans to close. It wasn't enough for small businesses to submit applications. There were two additional required steps: One, applications needed to be approved by one or more of our bank partners, and two, when applications were approved, small businesses needed to accept the loan.

Unfortunately, these latter two steps weren't going according to plan. Given the large number of banks we were working with, we assumed that half of all applications would be approved. The actual result was only 20 percent. We had also assumed that half of the approved applications would successfully convert into loans. The actual result was again 20 percent. And we had assumed that the average loan size would be $20,000. But the actual amount was $7,500.

Putting it all together, we had assumed that for every 1,000 applications we received, we would generate $5 million in loans. In actual practice, we were generating $300,000.

So we attacked the issue from every angle. We tried to identify banks with more permissive underwriting standards. We tried to partner with a broader set of banks. We tried to improve the usability of our website so that loan conversion rates would rise. We tried to target small businesses with stronger credit. We tried to target small businesses that needed larger loans. We even explored the possibility of becoming a lender ourselves.

We did everything we could think of to improve our results, but were only marginally successful. The truth, though distressing, was undeniable: Without a dramatic change in strategy, we were on the road to ruin.

Our fundamental challenge was adverse selection.

At the turn of the 21st century, the internet was still a novelty, and many people were uncomfortable sharing financial information online. As a result, most small business owners still preferred to apply for loans in person. We were well aware of this obstacle from the start, but believed – based on customer research – that there would be enough early adopters to build a viable business. It was a calculated bet, and we were wrong. It turned out that the vast majority of small business applicants on our site had been rejected for loans by their local banks. They weren't creditworthy, and desperation was their only reason for applying online. Meanwhile, the subset of small business applicants that were creditworthy had a lot of offline alternatives.

In late 2001, I grudgingly accepted reality. I decided to give up on small business lending, conserve cash by laying off more than half the team, and shift to an entirely new strategy.

Five years later, OnDeck Capital was founded in New York City. The company was devoted to revolutionizing small business lending. Small business owners could apply online for loans and get an immediate response. While OnDeck's approach wasn't identical to ours, the similarities far outweighed the differences. OnDeck Capital grew very rapidly and eventually went public.

I had mixed emotions when I heard about OnDeck's IPO. On the one hand, their success validated our original concept. On the other hand, it was a painful reminder of lost opportunity. Our idea had been sound, and our execution was generally strong, but we were five years too early.

Timing is everything.

FEELING LUCKY?

Timing may be everything, but luck also plays a major role. People tend to discount the significance of luck because we want to believe that we control our own destiny. Many of the most famous adages about luck reflect this sensibility. For example, "Luck is an accident that happens to the competent." Or, "I am a great believer in luck, and I find the harder I work, the more I have of it."

In my experience, sometimes we can create our own luck. But often, things just happen.

When I was a 20-year-old college senior, I interviewed on campus to be a business analyst at McKinsey & Company. It was the first time I had ever interviewed for a corporate job, and I was woefully unprepared. I generally understood what McKinsey did, but knew almost nothing specific about the firm. I didn't even know where their offices were located.

The interview went poorly for the first 15 minutes. The interviewer, an associate from the New York City office, looked exhausted and bored. He had been interviewing my classmates continuously for two days and seemed mentally checked out. He was merely going through the motions and showed very little interest in anything I was saying.

Then everything changed when he asked, "What are your life goals?" My answer seemed to take him by surprise. I don't recall my exact words, but they were something to the following effect: "I want to live an interesting life. I'd like to travel a lot. I'd like to live in several different countries. I'd like to get married and have a family. And I'd like to be a serial entrepreneur." When I had finished speaking, he tilted his head and gave me a funny look. I wasn't sure what to make of it. Was my answer somehow unusual? Was he questioning my sincerity? Forty years later, I still don't know what caused him to have that reaction.

But whatever the reason, it prompted me to double down. I leaned forward, jabbed my index finger down onto the table between us, and emphatically declared, "That's not bullshit." And in that moment, my life changed forever. The interviewer, energized by my comment, suddenly came to life. He stared at me intently and became highly engaged. When our discussion concluded 10 minutes later, it was clear that things had gone well. I ended up getting the job.

As a result, I was hired for a summer job in Australia two years later because the recruiter was impressed that I had worked for McKinsey. As a result, I met my wife in Melbourne. As a result, I have two terrific, now fully grown, kids (Alex and Talia).

> **In other words, saying "bullshit" in an interview completely altered the trajectory of my life. But it wasn't planned. It didn't reflect hard work or competence. It was a spontaneous reaction. It was random. It was luck.**

I've seen similar luck-driven dynamics, on many occasions, as a CEO. Things just happen. Sometimes the outcome is good, and sometimes the outcome is bad. Sometimes the outcome initially appears to be good but ends up being bad in the end. Sometimes the outcome initially appears to be bad but ends up being good in the end.

Here are two examples. In my second stint as a CEO, I ran a fintech company named Tempo with the mission of revolutionizing the debit card industry. Debit cards have always been issued by people's banks. If, for example, you have a checking account at Bank of America, then Bank of

America issues you a debit card connected to that checking account. The concept behind Tempo, however, was to enable retailers to issue debit cards. The cards were still connected to people's bank accounts, but financial settlement was enabled through the electronic, bank-to-bank payment network known as the Automated Clearing House.

The benefit to retailers was that this approach significantly improved their economics. Payment networks like Visa and Mastercard charge fees every time a debit card is used. A large percentage of these fees is paid to the bank that issued the card. By disintermediating banks, our company enabled retailers to meaningfully reduce costs. And some of these savings were invested in customer loyalty programs that helped to generate higher sales.

It was a complicated business, but a compelling proposition. After several years of struggle, we started to make rapid progress. We signed deals with many of America's leading gas station and convenience store chains. We forged strategic relationships with Mastercard and Discover. Walmart expressed interest in working with us. In less than 12 months, our revenue run rate skyrocketed from nearly nothing to more than $30 million. We were on our way.

Then fate intervened. The United States Congress was getting close to passing the Dodd-Frank Act. This new legislation was a response to the Great Recession of 2008 and was intended to strengthen regulatory oversight of America's financial system. Shortly before the final vote was scheduled to be taken, Senator Dick Durbin of Illinois introduced an amendment focused on debit cards. His objective was to impose price controls on debit card transaction fees so that retailers would save money.

And just like that, Congress effectively legislated our business model out of existence. The "Durbin Amendment" was approved. The Dodd-Frank Act became law. And retailers no longer needed a new type of debit card to reduce their transactional fees. We were toast.

Was there anything we could have done to avert this development? No. It was luck. Bad luck.

Ten years later, I was running an innovative background-checking company named Inflection, and things were going well. We had a run rate of more than $25 million, revenues were growing more than 40 percent per year, and we had achieved breakeven. It was at this point that one of our board members made a seemingly bizarre suggestion. He encouraged us to consider taking the company public in Australia. At first impression, this idea made no sense. All of the company's customers were in the United States, and we had no business presence whatsoever in Australia. But, based on my background, I took the idea seriously. My wife is from Australia. Our kids are dual citizens of Australia and the United States. I've lived in Australia several times. Upon reflection, the concept didn't seem entirely absurd.

I did some research and quickly concluded that the concept wasn't absurd at all. For various reasons, Australian investors were highly receptive to US-based technology companies going public on the Australian Securities Exchange (ASX). Moreover, relative to American investors, Australian investors would value us much higher. We had recently received (and rejected) an acquisition offer in the States for nearly US$100 million. It appeared that going public in Australia would deliver a valuation three times this amount. The answer seemed obvious. There was a window of opportunity, but it wasn't clear how long it would remain open, and so we needed to move fast.

A blur of frenetic activity ensued. Over the next six months, we retained bankers, traveled around Australia briefing prospective investors, overhauled our board of directors, introduced a series of mind-numbing systems and processes to ensure regulatory compliance, drafted a prospectus, and scheduled our road show. We were about three months away from ringing the bell at the ASX in Sydney. Then COVID-19 hit.

And just like that, the window closed. By the time it reopened nine months later, valuations had dramatically declined. Now going public in Australia would yield a valuation of only US$150 million, a 50 percent haircut from the original estimate. And that assumed the IPO would succeed. Investor interest in our company had significantly diminished despite our continued progress. The conclusion was unavoidable: The IPO was off.

It was luck again – apparently bad luck. But then, a short time later, when a large prospective acquirer unexpectedly contacted us, we realized that it was actually good luck. They were willing to pay a premium, and we ended up selling the business for US$400 million.

In the words of American short story writer Bret Harte, "The only sure thing about luck is that it will change."[5]

WHAT, ME WORRY?

Life as a CEO is enormously stressful, and the stress is multidimensional.

First, it's a lot of responsibility. The decisions you make have a direct impact on people's lives. And it's not only employees whose lives are affected, but also their families' lives. You may not have met most of your employees' partners and kids, but you know they're out there, and they're all depending on you to do a great job. It's a heavy burden.

Second, you constantly need to make judgments based on limited information. In other words, the job depends on a lot of guesswork. They may be educated guesses. The guesses may be analytically based and thoughtfully made. They may reflect years of experience and pattern recognition. But it's guesswork nonetheless. And consequently, many of the decisions you make are wrong.

In addition, everything you do is scrutinized and magnified: the decisions you make, your body language, how you interact with people on the team, what you say in meetings, emails, and on Slack, and how you say it. So you need to be hypervigilant at all times. You don't want to be misinterpreted. You don't want to create confusion. You don't want to accidentally damage someone's morale. And you certainly don't want to reveal any anxiety or lack of confidence that you might be experiencing. It's exhausting.

> **It's also intensely lonely. You are part of a team yet isolated from it. You constantly communicate with people – employees, investors, customers – about a wide range of topics, but not about how you are doing personally. Your job is to focus on other people. It's about them, not about you. And so you often struggle in silence.**

Furthermore, startups are intrinsically turbulent. Things go well and poorly in a random sequence. Sometimes a day starts out good and ends up bad. Sometimes a day starts out bad and ends up good. At 10 a.m., you're on top of the world. At 2 p.m., you're facing existential peril. The only thing predictable is unpredictability. Murphy's Law reigns supreme.

And through it all, you are both the captain and a passenger. You may be the boss, but it's your employees who do most of the work, especially as companies grow. And that too is stressful because it further reinforces your lack of control. I'm reminded of a conversation I had some years ago with Brad Smith, then CEO of Intuit. He observed, "Everyone thinks that I have a lot of power, but I really don't. I'm entirely dependent on other people. I can't make anybody do anything."

KEEPING IT TOGETHER

Through the years, I've developed two main coping strategies for CEO-related stress management. The first is never to get too high or too low. Whenever something good happens, I always assume that something bad is just around the corner. Whenever something bad happens, I always assume that something good is just around the corner. In other words, I am neither an optimist nor a pessimist. I am both at the same time. This approach has served me well, although it has a significant drawback. It's hard to enjoy the moment if you are always waiting for the other shoe to drop.

My second coping strategy is to focus on input rather than outcome. This is inherently challenging because we live in a world obsessed with outcomes. In college and professional sports, for example, all that anybody cares about are wins and losses. Winning is synonymous with success, and losing is synonymous with failure. The same framework applies in the business world. In the end, it's all about results. And the most important results are financial. What is the company's revenue? What is the growth rate? How about cash flow and profitability? What ROI will investors ultimately receive? That's how success is determined. The outcome is everything.

> **But the outcome isn't controllable. Consequently, worrying about the outcome, while sometimes unavoidable, isn't helpful in the slightest. It's a waste of time, a waste of energy, and a significant distraction. And it's emotionally draining.**

The better approach is to focus 100 percent on the things you can actually control. For example, who is on the team? How motivated are they? How hard are they working? How effectively are they working? Is money being intelligently spent? Have processes and systems been developed that will enable the company to scale? And more tangibly, are customers happy with the product? Has product-market fit been achieved? How well-designed is the technology platform? How impactful is the marketing?

This type of input-focused approach has two important benefits. It helps you maintain your emotional equilibrium when adversity inevitably strikes. And, ironically, it almost always yields a better outcome in the end.

It's a real-life application of the Serenity Prayer. "God, grant me the serenity to accept the things I cannot change, the courage to change the things I can, and the wisdom to know the difference."

WHAT'S THE STORY?

I had two misconceptions when my son initially enrolled in film school at NYU. The first was that the primary purpose of film school is to teach students how movies are made. The second was that the main lessons he would learn would have little connection to my experience as a CEO. I was wrong on both counts.

Alex attended NYU for three semesters before transferring to the USC School of Cinematic Arts. Then, after graduation, he went to work for Academy Award–winning director Ron Howard. Over the next four years, Alex assisted Ron on three feature-length films: *Thirteen Lives*, *Hillbilly Elegy*, and *Rebuilding Paradise*. And what he learned from Ron echoed what he had learned from his professors at NYU and USC: When it comes to making movies, storytelling is the most important priority. If you can't tell a compelling story, then you can't make a compelling movie.

As a CEO, you have three primary roles, and each is roughly equal in importance. First, and most obviously, you're a business leader. You're responsible for setting strategy and managing company operations. Second, you're a psychologist. You're constantly in the mode of asking a lot of questions and listening closely to the answers. If you want to motivate the people on your team, you need a nuanced understanding of what makes them tick. And third, just like folks in the film industry, you're a storyteller. You have to be proficient at telling stories or your company is much less likely to succeed.

To be clear, when I refer to storytelling, I'm not suggesting you should make things up. The stories I have in mind aren't works of fiction. I believe that CEOs should tell the truth. What I'm talking about, instead, is the ability to explain things to people so that what you're communicating resonates with them both intellectually and emotionally.

The "stories" that you tell – and the way you tell them – are affected by a wide range of variables. For example, your audience is a key consideration. Are you communicating with employees, job applicants, existing customers, prospective customers, investors, or some other constituency? Your motivation for telling the story is also highly significant. Are you hoping to convince people to do something that they aren't required to do, like invest in the company or buy the company's product? Or are you looking to inspire, reassure, or simply inform? Moreover, the tone of the story is critical. Are you sharing good news, bad news, or something in between? And how will the story be conveyed? Are you generating a slide deck, crafting an email, drafting a DM in Slack, or preparing a verbal presentation? If you want your story to be as effective as possible, you need to take all of these various elements into account.

In this context, one of my pet peeves is the way that most people, including most CEOs, create presentations in Google Slides or PowerPoint. Their process, in my opinion, is ass-backward. They immediately rush into creating slides without first developing a clear and effective narrative. As a result, the message – assuming there is one – ends up getting muddled. The "plot" is hard to follow.

I prefer to do the exact opposite. I start by asking myself, "What's the story?" Once the answer is clear in my mind, I write one or more paragraphs that cohesively articulate the narrative. I then extract each of the individual sentences I've written and copy them onto separate blank slides. And then, and only then, do I start building out the deck, making sure the content for each slide and the sentence for that slide closely align. It's a far better approach because it ensures that what you're trying to communicate is easier to understand and meaningfully more impactful.

> **My preoccupation with slide creation aside, the larger point is that telling stories is a fundamental part of the job. In the words of the old Hopi proverb: "Those who tell the stories rule the world." That applies equally to Hollywood directors and Silicon Valley CEOs.**

AFTER ALL, WE ARE NOT COMMUNISTS

I decided to pursue an entrepreneurial career in Silicon Valley for reasons that had nothing to do with money. It was partly an artistic impulse. I wanted to work on things that were creative and new. I was excited about innovation and the potential for disrupting the status quo.

It was partly a desire for independence and autonomy. I wanted to chart my own destiny, take control of my professional life, and avoid becoming a bureaucratic cog. As a 13-year-old, I was inspired by the British TV show, *The Prisoner*, in which the protagonist stubbornly declares, "I am not a number. I am a free man!"[6] That defiant sensibility has always resonated with me.

And I hoped to make a positive social contribution. I liked the idea of devoting my time and effort to improving people's lives.

That isn't to say I didn't care about making money. It just wasn't my top priority.

No, my career goals were mainly aspirational. And 30 years later, I feel the same way. I've met a lot of folks in Silicon Valley who are similarly inclined. Some derive energy from building products and solving complex problems. Others enjoy helping customers and collaborating with peers. The common theme is that money isn't their primary motivation.

> **But make no mistake about it, while many Silicon Valley companies have aspirational missions and aspirational visions and are populated by aspirationally motivated employees, they are ruled by money. They are capitalistic to the core.**

And the people, like me, who run these companies, are agents of capitalism. I say that unapologetically. It is simply the truth. In the words of Don Barzini from *The Godfather*: "After all, we are not communists."[7]

IT'S ABOUT THE MONEY

I had the privilege of being mentored for nearly a decade by a fellow named Bill Campbell. Bill was a remarkable human being: razor-sharp, perceptive, charismatic, and kind. Many of the most important lessons that I learned about being a CEO, I learned from Bill.

Bill had an unusual backstory. He initially pursued a career as a college football coach, spending six years as an assistant coach at Boston College and five years as head coach at his alma mater, Columbia University. Then, nearing 40, he decided to make a significant change and reinvent himself as a businessman. His trajectory was meteoric. Within several years, he was VP of marketing at Apple. A few years later, he became a first-time CEO. And half a decade after that, he was hired as CEO of Intuit.

But his greatest impact came after his time as a CEO. By his early 60s, Bill had quietly become a powerful force in Silicon Valley and beyond. Broadly revered for his judgment, character, and gravitas, Bill became unofficially known as the "Coach of Silicon Valley." He was simultaneously chairman of Intuit, the most influential board member at Apple, the most influential advisor at Google, and chairman of Columbia's Board of Trustees. He actively advised many of the most prominent tech industry leaders of the time, including Steve Jobs, Jeff Bezos, Sergey Brin, Larry Page, Eric Schmidt, and Sheryl Sandberg. And he, nonetheless, placed equal emphasis on advising many less prominent CEOs and entrepreneurs. I was incredibly fortunate to be one of these people.

Bill was exceptionally compassionate and empathetic. He didn't just give lip service to caring about others; he genuinely meant it. And his leadership philosophy reflected this perspective. His approach was emphatically people-centric. He thought that treating people well was an end in and of itself, but also resulted in substantially better team performance.

Perhaps the most famous quote from *The Godfather* is, "It's not personal, it's strictly business."[8] I think Bill would have disagreed. For Bill, business was always intensely personal.

Yet Bill was no starry-eyed idealist. He was pragmatic and realistic about the context in which he operated. He knew he was an agent of capitalism, although the topic was never openly discussed. It was implicit. As much as he cared about people, and he did – intensely – his objective was to help build great companies. And in the end, that meant financial considerations were of paramount importance.

"It's not about the money," Bill would forcefully declare. Then, with a twinkle in his eye, he would dramatically pause before finishing the thought. "It's about the fucking money!"

It was a great line, and it always made me laugh. But it was also a useful admonition. Bill wasn't just trying to be funny; he was making a critical point.

> **A business that runs out of money goes out of business. A business that doesn't generate much revenue doesn't survive very long. And, especially in Silicon Valley, a business that doesn't produce consistent revenue growth rapidly fizzles out. While this all sounds obvious, it's very easy to forget, or at least neglect, when you are consumed with the tactical daily frenzy of running a company.**

There is also a great temptation for CEOs to excessively focus on the functional areas that we know most about. If your background is in sales, you're likely to overemphasize sales. If your background is in product management, you're likely to overemphasize product management. And so on. This isn't surprising. It's our comfort zone. We naturally gravitate to topics where we have the most knowledge, can add the most value, and that interest us the most. But this is a perilous approach. When we devote too much time and energy to certain areas, we devote too little time and energy to others. While there are certainly exceptions to the rule, most technology CEOs weren't finance professionals earlier in their careers. And so "the money" can be easy to neglect.

My fourth company, named SugarSync, was a file hosting service that competed with Dropbox. SugarSync was founded first, but Dropbox, after creating a product that was more intuitive and easier to use, quickly established a dominant market position. Meanwhile, SugarSync's revenue, which had been growing at a solid pace for several years, suddenly plateaued and then started to slide. My predecessor as SugarSync's CEO tried valiantly to reverse this trend. But she applied most of her efforts to marketing and public relations because those were her areas of expertise. The board of directors ultimately replaced her because they believed that the company's product and technology were the areas of greatest weakness. Unfortunately, amidst all of the drama – declining revenue, an excessive focus on marketing and PR, a lack of strategic alignment between the CEO and the board of directors, and a disruptive change in CEO – no one was paying attention to the company's rapidly diminishing bank balance. By the time I joined, the company was running on fumes, with only six weeks of remaining cash. Yet no one had noticed.

In the end, we survived and lived to fight another day. In the nick of time, our investors provided just enough funding to pull us back from the abyss. While the company still faced an existential crisis, the lesson was clear.

Yes, a comprehensive turnaround was required, with significant changes to product, technology platform, and marketing alike. However, nothing was more important than the fucking money.

IT'S ABOUT THE PEOPLE

What is a company? ChatGPT describes it as a legal entity that produces goods and services. Most of us would provide a similar response. If asked, for example, "What is Apple?," the typical answer would focus on iPhones, iPads, Macs, and AirPods. That's understandable. We tend to think of companies based on what they do.

But that confuses the forest for the trees. The larger truth is that a company is synonymous with the people who work for it. The people are the company because, without them, there is no company.

Let's imagine that Thanos, mortal enemy of the Avengers, actually exists. And let's further imagine that for reasons known only to Thanos, he prefers Windows, Android, Dell, and Samsung, and despises all things related to Apple. As a result, after collecting all six Infinity Stones, he decides to promptly wield his power by punishing Apple. He snaps his fingers and all of Apple's employees spontaneously disappear.

The business consequence? Apple ceases to exist.

Back in the real world, of course, Apple continues to thrive. As it has for many years, it continues making products that generally delight customers (irrespective of what Thanos might think). But these products don't magically appear. They don't generate themselves. Great products only exist because talented people created them. Talented people are the essential ingredient.

So yes, it's about the fucking money, but it's likewise about the people. I'm reminded of the question once posed by my friend (LiveCapital co-founder) Scott Belser: "What's more important? Your heart or your lungs?" If the answer isn't apparent, you need both to survive.

THE TWO GOLDEN RULES

My first entrepreneurial venture had nothing to do with computer technology. It was a T-shirt company that I co-founded with Joel Getz, my best friend from college. Our business model involved licensing artwork, screen printing the licensed images onto T-shirts, and then wholesaling the shirts to retail stores. Customers included Bloomingdale's, Saks Fifth Avenue, Macy's, and a plethora of smaller chains and boutiques that, thanks to the internet, largely no longer exist.

The company had two main product lines: one devoted to indigenous Australian art, the other featuring the work of renowned American illustrator Norman Rockwell. Both lines performed equally well, but a specific Rockwell image, *The Golden Rule*, was by far our best seller.

The Golden Rule was originally painted in 1961. A mosaic version was later created for permanent display at the United Nations. The work is a compelling reminder of our common humanity. It's an image of people from around the world standing shoulder to shoulder, in quiet solidarity. And the shared aspiration that unifies the group is reflected in the Golden Rule. The words are inscribed in the middle of the image: "Do unto others as you would have them do unto you."

> **I'm an idealist at heart, so the Golden Rule has always resonated with me. But, of course, idealism doesn't always prevail. We live in a world where people routinely mistreat one another, and decisions are often based on self-interest and power dynamics rather than morality or ethics. Thus, there is a second Golden Rule that frequently applies: "They who have the gold make the rules."**

When you're running a company in Silicon Valley, these two Golden Rules sometimes collide. And when such conflict arises, you may be forced to make some uncomfortable choices that test – and perhaps clarify – your personal values.

I launched my first Silicon Valley startup with a different friend: Scott Belser. Scott and I had talked for many years about co-founding a company. Finally, the moment had arrived. We identified a concept that we were excited about and decided to take the plunge. The timing seemed ideal. The dot-com boom was in full swing, with internet investment exploding. We moved quickly to create a PowerPoint deck and begin fundraising.

I don't remember who introduced us to the Band of Angels, a group of wealthy Silicon Valley luminaries looking to invest in new and innovative high-tech startups. But I know that the introduction was made only a few days after we started the company. The following week, Scott and I met at my San Francisco apartment with one of the group's co-founders, Hans Severiens. The meeting went well, and Hans soon introduced us to several additional members of the Band. One of the men, Ron Conway, was particularly enthusiastic about our idea.

In the ensuing years, Ron would establish himself as one of the preeminent angel investors in Silicon Valley. At the time, however, Ron was new to investing. He was a former operating executive and had both public company and entrepreneurial experience as a CEO. Coincidentally, Ron and I had first crossed paths two years earlier, shortly after I joined Intuit. We had discussed the possibility of forming a strategic alliance between Intuit and the company he had founded, Personal Training Systems. Although the two of us got along well, the alliance never came to fruition. The following year, Ron sold his company.

Our discussions with the Band of Angels rapidly advanced. Mainly due to Ron's proactive involvement, many members decided to invest. We lined up commitments for more than $500,000 in less than a week. Scott and I were amazed and delighted with the rate of progress. Fundraising was proving to be much easier than we had anticipated. Or so we believed.

The dynamics began to shift during our next meeting with Ron, a conversation that was, for the most part, uneventful. It focused on the logistical steps that needed to be completed for the round to close. But then, with the meeting winding down, Ron asked a question that took us by surprise: "Which of you is going to be the CEO?" My answer, in turn, took Ron by surprise: "We actually weren't thinking that way. We're business partners, and we've been planning to run the business together." Ron was quiet for a moment and furrowed his brow. Then he shook his head. "No. There needs to be a CEO."

We got the message. We committed to promptly getting back to Ron with a definitive response, and, with that, the meeting ended. But we were uncertain about next steps. I had meant what I said to Ron, even if it sounded hopelessly naive to him. There had been no CEO in the T-shirt company I co-founded. While my business partner and I had different responsibilities, we ran the company as equals. I had mistakenly assumed that the same approach would be acceptable in Silicon Valley.

The challenge that Scott and I faced was that neither of us wanted to be CEO. We were interested in being entrepreneurs and building a company together. Lofty titles and corporate hierarchy didn't appeal to us. Consequently, when we discussed what to do, each of us suggested that the other was the better fit. In the end, my argument won the day. I asserted that Scott would be regarded as the stronger choice because he was 16 years older and had many more years of professional experience. Scott half-heartedly agreed.

Unfortunately, Ron didn't react the way we had hoped. He accepted the decision, but only as a short-term solution. He replied with passive-aggressive civility, "OK, that's fine. But after we close the round, I think we need to look for a new, permanent CEO." Scott and I were stunned by this comment and weren't sure what to say in response. We exchanged a brief, knowing glance and remained silent.

Once Ron departed, however, we had a lot to talk about. The situation was quickly getting out of hand. Scott and I had aspired to go into business together for nearly a decade. Now, only six weeks after creating a slide deck, we were losing control of our company before it even existed. We decided to politely, but firmly, push back. It fell to Scott, as our newly designated CEO, to deliver the message.

We reconvened with Ron the following day, and the meeting was a train wreck. As Scott expressed our resistance to hiring a new CEO, Ron became quickly antagonized. He seemed to regard the feedback as a personal affront and declared in no uncertain terms that, given our attitude, the deal was off. And with that, he stormed out of the room.

It was an upsetting and bewildering turn of events. Scott blamed himself for Ron's reaction, but I disagreed. I thought Scott had been direct but diplomatic, and that Ron had overreacted. Regardless, our situation had suddenly become precarious. The Band of Angels was extremely well connected. Losing their investment was only the tip of the iceberg. If they decided to badmouth us, we might not be able to raise money from anybody.

Neither of us had any idea what to do. We returned to the small office that we had recently started using, and spent the next several hours feeling sorry for ourselves. Scott looked grim and despondent. I silently contemplated whether leaving my job had been a mistake. The minutes passed slowly. And then, the phone rang. It was Ron. He asked me to meet with him at his house in Atherton as soon as possible, and I reluctantly agreed. I arrived about 20 minutes later.

We sat down on opposite sides of Ron's dining room table, and Ron immediately cut to the chase. He said, "Look, I know that was a tough meeting. But here's the thing. I think Scott is trouble, and I'm not willing to work with him. I would, however, like to work with you. So here's what I propose: You become the CEO. You stop working with Scott. And we'll fund the company."

When I look back at that moment, I hesitate to describe it as an ethical dilemma. That isn't the way I experienced it because the answer seemed so obvious. I wasn't going to walk away from Scott. I don't abandon people, and I don't stab anyone in the back, even when I barely know them. I would certainly never behave that way with one of my closest friends. The Golden Rule – the traditional version – really does mean something to me.

In addition, I also knew that Ron had misjudged the situation. His impression of Scott was simply wrong. Scott is an exceptional human being. He is super smart, extremely diligent, highly ethical, fun to be around, and very easy to work with. It was clear, to me at least, that we would make an excellent team.

So, with as much politeness as I could muster, I rejected Ron's proposal. I told him that I appreciated his confidence in me, but that I wouldn't feel comfortable bailing on Scott. Ron didn't seem surprised or upset by my response. On the contrary, he seemed to respect what I was saying, even if he disagreed with it. He walked me to the door, shook my hand, and wished me well. And then I got into my aging Mazda and drove away.

The consequence of that decision: We couldn't raise money for the next two years. Viewed purely from a narrow, hard-nosed, business perspective, it was the wrong choice. But I never doubted my decision.

The point of this story is not that Ron is a villain. He isn't. In fact, I like him a lot. He is a force of nature – a whirling dervish of energy, intensity, charisma, enthusiasm, and speed. When Ron invests in a company, he is always forthright, helpful, and exceptionally responsive. And I know all of that because he was an investor in three of the companies I subsequently ran.

No, the point of the story is that the two Golden Rules sometimes clash with each other.

> **In my experience, most investors (including Ron) treat people well most of the time. They generally adhere to the traditional Golden Rule. But their primary objective isn't optimizing for the traditional Golden Rule – it's maximizing their financial return. They have the gold and want more of it. That's the reason they make investments.**

That's the reason venture capital exists. And because they have the gold, they have considerable influence. Now and then, they may conclude that maximizing financial return requires exerting that influence and changing the rules of engagement. They may decide to do unto others what they would not want done unto them.

I returned to the office and gave Scott the update. He responded stoically but was clearly shaken up. While he appreciated that I had stuck by him, he felt badly about the feedback Ron had provided and the situation we now found ourselves in. It had been a very difficult day.

The drama ended as abruptly as it began, but there were two lasting consequences. First, the crisis brought us closer together, and the strength of that bond proved critical as the months and years progressed. And second, we decided that I should be the company's CEO.

LIVES OVER LIVELIHOODS

More than half of Inflection's engineers lived in Ukraine, and I grew increasingly apprehensive. The previous year, Vladimir Putin had deployed many thousands of Russian soldiers near Ukraine's border. Then, over the past several weeks, the deployment had dramatically intensified. One hundred and fifty thousand heavily armed troops were now in position – to the north, south, and east of Ukraine – and were poised to attack. The situation seemed perilous and grim. At least, that was my impression. The team in Ukraine, however, wasn't convinced.

For the second time in three months, I scheduled a mandatory Zoom call to discuss the situation. My message was blunter than it had been in our initial meeting. I told them that since an invasion appeared imminent, the company would financially enable them, along with their families, to leave Ukraine until things settled down. We would find them a place to live in a different part of Europe and fund all of their incremental travel and living costs. There was precedent for this suggestion. Back in 2014, when Russia annexed Crimea and war broke out in the Donbas, most of the team had been hastily relocated to Montenegro at the company's expense. They spent six months as expats before it was deemed safe to return home. While that event predated my arrival at Inflection by several years, I was well aware of the history. And I thought that the company had a moral obligation to rise to the occasion once more.

I spoke for about five minutes, and everyone listened respectfully. But when they finally responded, the feedback wasn't what I expected to hear. The prevailing view – expressed politely – was that I was overreacting, and that while they appreciated my concern, they didn't share it. They believed that Putin was only saber-rattling and that invasion was unlikely. Only two people expressed any interest in my proposal.

I wasn't sure what to think. I was only reading about the conflict from half a world away, while they were living in the middle of it. What did I know? Maybe they were right. Yet I wondered whether distance might be providing me with a clearer perspective. The "boiling frog syndrome" came to mind – the famous metaphor about the frog that, after being placed into lukewarm water, is gradually cooked to death. I also recalled a provocative question that my father had once posed when I was a teenager. He asked me, "If you were living in Nazi Germany during the mid-1930s, would you – someone with Jewish heritage – have correctly assessed the danger and gotten out in time? Or would you have taken a more patient approach, and then waited until it was too late to leave?" On the call, however, I didn't mention either of these philosophical ruminations. I concluded that it wouldn't be appropriate or effective for me to try to force the issue. Despite my misgivings, there was nothing further I could do. If people weren't willing to leave, even for a short time, that was their prerogative – for better or worse.

It proved to be worse. Russia invaded the following week.

Thankfully, no one on the team was killed or wounded. But the invasion severely disrupted their lives. Some immediately fled west from Kyiv, aiming to reach Poland, Slovakia, or Romania. Several of the women were able to leave the country unhindered. Most of the men, however, were stopped at the border after Ukraine declared martial law. One of the women crossed into Poland with her two-year-old son, but her husband was forced to remain in Ukraine, and in the midst of all the confusion and mayhem, their cat ran away and was lost. Another woman decided at the last moment not to cross into Poland when it became clear that her husband wouldn't be allowed to join her. Others, meanwhile, hunkered down in the city, hiding in their apartments, or sheltering in metro stations and makeshift bomb shelters.

A few hours after the invasion started, our head of technology created a WhatsApp group to facilitate communication. Nonetheless, we quickly lost touch with about a third of the team. In a few cases, it took more than a week to confirm their safety.

I've never felt more helpless as a CEO. Our options were limited. As far as I could tell, the only assistance we could provide – beyond some heartfelt expressions of moral support – was financial. We wanted to ensure that people continued receiving their pay. Moreover, a few folks needed additional financial support. Ironically, even in this situation, Bill Campbell's admonition ("It's not about the money; it's about the fucking money") still applied, in a way that he had never anticipated, but would have fully embraced.

Through it all, our Ukrainian team found a way to keep diligently working, despite persistent power outages, frequent loss of internet access, and many other significant logistical and emotional challenges. And they kept working even when we encouraged them to take days off. I've never been more impressed by a group of people.

As I look back at that experience, three lessons stand out. The first is that black swan events ("rare, unpredictable occurrences with severe consequences"[9]) are an unavoidable part of business – and life. Second, if you hire the right people, and they're confronted with extreme adversity, they're capable of extraordinary courage and resolve. Third, and most profoundly, some things transcend business. In the bigger picture, lives are more important than livelihoods.

A FOOL AND THEIR MONEY ARE SOON PARTED

There is an old adage, typically attributed to Benjamin Franklin, that "In this world, nothing is certain other than death and taxes." Of course, Benjamin Franklin never had the chance to work in Silicon Valley. If he had, he might have added a third component: "In this world, nothing is certain other than death, taxes, and stupidly excessive company spending."

> **As a general rule, venture-funded Silicon Valley companies waste a tremendous amount of money.**

There are a variety of reasons for this. First, in the immediate aftermath of a new funding round, it's easy to get carried away. All of a sudden, the company is flush with cash. The unaffordable has become affordable overnight. Then the feeding frenzy begins, and everyone starts coming out of the woodwork with requests for new spending.

In isolation, the requests generally sound reasonable: new headcount, new laptops, new subscription services, more money for marketing, more money for company events, more money for continuing education, higher salaries. However, in the aggregate, they're untenable.

So you try to mitigate the issue by encouraging everyone to treat the company's money as if it's their own. That's a nice-sounding slogan, but human nature presents a challenge: Most employees don't think that way, regardless of what you tell them. To paraphrase Tom Peters, "No one washes a rental car."[10] Furthermore, many folks are irresponsible when it comes to managing their personal finances. The last thing you want is for those people to treat the company's money as if it's their own.

Next, you establish financial controls and try to set limits on new spending. These are essential steps, but they don't necessarily solve the issue. Unless you're careful, financial controls end up too lax, and spending limits tend to be only sporadically enforced. The reason is that when new funding comes in, people feel irrationally exuberant. A deposit of millions of dollars tends to have that impact. And that feeling of irrational exuberance is often shared by the CEO, who has devoted the past several months to closing the round.

Moreover, as a CEO, you like it when employees feel passionate and motivated. You want to empower proactivity and a sense of urgency. Thus, when spending opportunities arise, there is a natural temptation to say yes. It's more fun and a lot easier to be Santa Claus than the Grinch.

> **Unfortunately, once you allow costs to rise, it becomes very tough to bring them back down. It's an easy mistake to make, but a rookie mistake nonetheless.**

Overhiring is a particularly big risk, and it's not only a function of irrational exuberance. There is an illusion that hiring more people naturally leads to greater progress. But it doesn't really work that way.

The theory seems to make sense. Let's say you have a 20-person team and then double it to 40. Shouldn't it be possible to get twice as much done? Well, not exactly. Communication and project planning are harder with a larger team, and consequently, more meetings are required as well as additional bureaucratic overhead. So shouldn't it be possible to get 75 percent more done? Well, not exactly. In fact, not even close. In my experience, if you hire the right people, doubling the team might increase productivity by 30–40 percent. And if you hire the wrong people, productivity will almost certainly decline.

Conspicuous consumption is an additional risk. While that's a term usually applied to consumers, it can have equal relevance in an entrepreneurial context. I'm referring to large expenditures on items that superficially seem exciting or glamorous but provide no actual business value. A common example: flying the entire team to Las Vegas for a two- to three-day company summit. Is it fun? Maybe. Some people will enjoy themselves. Is it worth the money? Not a chance. As the saying goes, "What happens in Vegas stays in Vegas." That is literally true for the money that gets wasted on these types of events. The money you spend in Vegas stays in Vegas. Whatever short-term benefit is achieved with respect to team building and morale immediately dissipates once the event is over.

Highway billboards are another example. When I was running my first company, LiveCapital, I was convinced to get a billboard on US 101, the main highway that runs through Silicon Valley. At the time, I thought it was a worthy investment. I wanted to let the Silicon Valley community know that we were on our way to building a great, transformative company. It was meant as a message for prospective investors and employees. And when the billboard was unveiled, I felt a surge of pride. We had struggled to navigate through the entrepreneurial wilderness for nearly four years, and had finally arrived.

It wasn't long before I started second-guessing myself. The billboard was costing us $75,000 per month, but there was no evidence that it was helping us to attract either new investors or new employees. I grudgingly came to realize that it was a complete and utter waste of money. It was an exorbitant exercise in vanity and nothing more. In the end, I had thoughtlessly pissed away nearly a quarter of a million dollars.

Nowadays, many years on, whenever I'm driving on US 101 and pass by a new billboard, I always think the same thing: I wonder who the inexperienced dumbass is who authorized that purchase. And then I remember that once upon a time, that inexperienced dumbass was me.

HAIL A TAXI

My father-in-law's best friend, Taufiq Harahap (Oom Taufiq), was an Indonesian tycoon. Between the 1960s and 1990s, he built a conglomerate that combined food and beverage (Indonesia's Coca-Cola franchise), electronics and telecommunications (Indonesia's Siemens franchise), and travel (Indonesia's largest travel agency). I met him a year after my father-in-law passed away, at our wedding in Boston. Four years later when Wati and I traveled to Jakarta, we stayed at his family's house.

I had the chance to speak with Oom Taufiq only once during our visit, but it was an extremely memorable conversation. He spent the first half hour telling me his backstory. I don't recall all the details, but I do remember that his first entrepreneurial venture involved selling guns during the Indonesian War of Independence. On one occasion, he was detained by soldiers and nearly executed, but figured out a way to talk himself out of trouble. After the war, he took the money he had earned from gun running and started investing in businesses that were safer and more conventional.

At this point in the narrative, he paused and looked at me intently. He said, "Do you want to know the secret of my success?" I nodded in response. He then shared the following allegory: "Sometimes you're driving in a car, and the car gets stuck in the mud. And so you try to get the car out of the mud. You rev the engine. You turn the wheel left and right. You switch gears. You put the car in reverse. And nothing works. The tires just spin uselessly, and the car gets ever more deeply embedded. So what do you do? Most people keep trying to get the car unstuck. I open the door, step out of the car, and hail a taxi."

Entrepreneurial companies frequently get stuck in the metaphorical mud. Periodically, they can extricate themselves through persistence and hard work. However, persistence and hard work aren't always sufficient. Often, the business model is the problem. And when it is, you have a Darwinian choice: adapt or die.

To be fair, it's not always obvious when the business model is the problem, especially early on. When progress is limited, sometimes execution is to blame rather than strategy. So how do you know when the issue is primarily strategic? It's a judgment call. But usually, when you have a smart and tenacious team, and your product isn't getting much traction, something is wrong with the strategy.

Early in my career, prior to moving to Silicon Valley, I worked in brand management at Johnson & Johnson. I was responsible for the two products focused on babies' bottoms: wipes and diaper rash ointment. The latter, Johnson's Baby Diaper Rash Relief, was a new initiative. It was, ostensibly, a major improvement over Desitin, the foul, fishy-smelling market leader. Our new product was objectively superior: It had been clinically proven to be more effective, was easier to apply due to its higher viscosity, and had an appealing scent.

Moreover, the product launch was supported by a $1 million-plus marketing campaign. We targeted two distinct customer segments (pediatricians and new parents), with a robust blend of print ads, public relations, price discounts, and in-store promotions. While brand management was a new experience for me, I felt very optimistic. Success seemed guaranteed.

But the universe had other ideas. I had assumed that our market position would rapidly improve. Instead, progress was glacial. After 90 days, our market share was only 3 percent. After an additional 90 days, it barely exceeded 5 percent.

My instinct was to double down, work even harder, and make some tactical adjustments. I thought that maybe our ad messaging had missed the mark. Or perhaps product packaging needed revision. Or possibly price discounts weren't sufficiently aggressive.

When I made these suggestions during a product review meeting, however, the VP of Marketing, Paul Michaels (who would later go on to become president of Mars Inc.), flatly disagreed. Instead of doubling down, he elected to eliminate the product's marketing budget – immediately. There was nothing to discuss or debate. He had made a decision, and that was final. Understandably, I was deflated, but Paul assured me that it wasn't my fault. In fact, he thought I had done a good job. Then, he shared with me what he described as his "seed parable."

"A farmer sows a field with seeds. The conditions seem ideal: healthy soil, an abundant water supply, and a temperate climate. Moreover, the farmer is diligent and skilled. Yet, for some reason, the seeds don't grow. Meanwhile, a different farmer sows a different field with a different set of seeds. This time, the conditions are practically apocalyptic: The soil is low in nutrients and high in salt, the area is in a state of perpetual drought, and, depending on time of day, the temperature wildly oscillates between extreme heat and extreme cold. And this farmer is lazy and inexperienced. Nonetheless, the seeds start growing." And with that, the meeting abruptly came to an end. Paul was a quirky guy.

However, his point was well taken.

> **Results can sometimes be surprising, even inexplicable, but they should never be ignored or mindlessly rationalized.**

In Paul's parable, Farmer #2 has identified an interesting opportunity, worthy of additional investment. Farmer #1 needs a new business model. It's time to hail a taxi and leave the farm.

THE BUSINESS MODEL IS NOT THE BUSINESS

Changing business models isn't so easy. First, it's operationally challenging. It's analogous to pulling a thread on a sweater. If you're not careful, the entire sweater will unravel.

For those who haven't experienced a business model change, its complexity is easy to underestimate. Why? Because the new and old business models are typically related, leading to considerable overlap. A company that helps large enterprises conduct background checks doesn't suddenly transform itself into a social media platform or online pharmacy. But it might shift its focus from large enterprises to small businesses. In other words, the old strategy isn't completely discarded, it's only "adjusted."

At first glance, the new and old business models may seem strikingly similar. In reality, however, they aren't. When, for example, you modify your target customer, it ripples through the entire business system, affecting sales motion, marketing messaging, financial metrics, product functionality, user interface, partnership strategy, hiring, etc. Strategic "adjustments" have far-reaching implications.

But the biggest challenge is usually emotional rather than operational. People often get emotionally attached to the original business model. As a result, changing the model can be disorienting and upsetting. Company founders are particularly susceptible to this reaction.

My second company (Tempo) started with a business model that combined three distinct elements: a new PIN debit network, a new type of debit card (decoupled debit) that relied on the Automated Clearing House (ACH) for settlement, and a new retailer-focused, debit card issuance platform. It was a bold and disruptive concept. We were trying to radically transform the American debit card industry, in direct competition with Visa, Mastercard, and the nation's largest banks. From the perspective of the founder, Scott Hatfield, it was more than just a business venture. It was a battle between good and evil. Based on his 15 years of experience in the debit card industry, Scott believed that banks and payment networks severely exploited retailers, particularly small retailers. Eventually, he decided to take action.

I was excited about the company's mission. The banks and payment networks really were acting in bad faith, and the prospect of taking them on strongly appealed to me. It was, to say the least, a high-risk, high-reward scenario. We faced powerful enemies, and our business model was an operational nightmare. And yet, we were doing something important, innovative, audaciously ambitious, and with enormous upside.

Over the next year, we made significant progress on two of our three strategic priorities: the ACH-enabled debit card and the issuance platform. However, our third key priority – creating a PIN debit network – was proving difficult. The challenge was that the PIN debit cards affiliated with Visa or Mastercard are accepted in the United States at more than a million locations. In order to successfully compete with Visa and Mastercard, we needed our debit network to be broadly accepted as well. We didn't expect our network to be comparably pervasive, at least not for many years, but we thought that getting to 600,000–700,000 accepting locations might be readily achievable.

Unfortunately, we were wrong. We grew to around 250,000 accepting locations relatively fast, but then progress slowed. It soon became apparent that getting to a critical mass would require too much money and too much time.

> **The business model needed to change. But how? The answer, though obvious, was heresy. We needed to switch sides. We needed to be Sith rather than Jedi. We needed to partner with Visa and Mastercard, or at least one of the two, instead of competing with them.**

The path forward required us to focus on the two parts of the business model that were working. Both retailers and customers liked decoupled debit. That was great news. But the only way to succeed was to work with an existing network.

To his credit, Scott supported the change. He understood why it was necessary. Nonetheless, he was severely disappointed. I told him, "We're going to be OK. The business model is not the business." And he looked back at me with a pained expression. I knew what it meant. The business would endure. But, for Scott, that was the day the dream died.

LESS IS MORE

Every time I've narrowed a company's strategic scope, the company has performed better. At Tempo, progress immediately accelerated when we walked away from building our own payment network. At Inflection, progress immediately accelerated when I shut down two of the company's three businesses.

The inverse has also been true. Every time I've expanded a company's strategic scope, the company has performed worse. At LiveCapital, we introduced the world's first online marketplace for small business lending. Then, a year later, I decided to create the world's first online marketplace for small business insurance. The result: slower progress in lending and minimal progress in insurance. It was only when I reversed course and shut down the insurance initiative – narrowing the company's strategic scope – that we began to regain momentum.

> **The lesson I've learned is that less is more. The challenge is that young companies – and the CEOs who run them – are naturally inclined to bite off more than they can chew.**

There are several reasons for this. First, the goal in Silicon Valley isn't building a nice little business. It's building a massive business that delivers an enormous ROI. The task is Herculean. As a result, it tends to attract people who are intrepid, have big ideas, and are supremely, or even pathologically, ambitious. This personality profile – type A on steroids – comes with a systemic bias: We try to do too much.

Second, entrepreneurship is precarious and daunting. It's reminiscent of a line from the James Bond film *Spectre*, "You're a kite dancing in a hurricane, Mr. Bond."[11] Founders and CEOs have a significant amount at stake – financially, psychologically, and reputationally. You're way out on a limb – you've left your job, taken a pay cut, hired people who are counting on you, and raised money from other people, often including friends and family, who are also counting on you. Given this daunting context, the desire to mitigate risk is hard to suppress. No matter how excited and optimistic you are about the business, putting all your eggs in one basket is unsettling. As a result, it's very tempting to look for ways to diversify. The result is scope creep.

It's also easy to be fooled into thinking that opportunities adjacent to your primary area of focus are natural extensions of your strategy. But that usually isn't the case. At LiveCapital, I made the mistake of thinking that small business insurance and small business lending were more similar than different. After all, both relied on a flexible decision engine and seemed tightly aligned in terms of target customer, marketing methodology, partnership dynamics, regulatory oversight, and product usability. In reality, however, the overlap was minimal. The similarities were only superficial. As I came to realize, the nuances of insurance and lending are entirely different. Expanding into insurance was one of the more boneheaded decisions that I've ever made.

Furthermore, feedback, however well intended, can be highly disruptive. It's a double-edged sword. On the one hand, it's absolutely vital to listen to your customers, employees, and investors with an open mind. They collectively know much more than you do individually, and their knowledge and insight are indispensable. On the other hand, it's essential not to overreact to what people tell you. You need to be highly selective about which feedback to act upon, or you can quickly lose your way.

I'm reminded of a scene from the 1960s television sitcom *Gilligan's Island*. The castaways, facing their latest existential crisis, are trying to determine who has been stealing food from their supply hut. The Professor offers a possible explanation, and Gilligan immediately responds, "You're right, Professor." A moment later, Ginger provides a different explanation, and Gilligan replies, "You're right, Ginger." Next, Maryanne suggests a third possibility, and once again Gilligan agrees, "You're right, Maryanne." At this point, the Skipper, annoyed, turns to Gilligan and chastises him, "Gilligan, everyone can't be right!" Gilligan pauses, reflects for a moment, nods his head, and then declares, "Skipper, you're right, too."[12]

> **Gilligan may not be the ideal role model for a Silicon Valley CEO, but if you aren't careful, it's very easy to behave like him, especially in the early days of a company's existence.**

You have a business concept, but it's neither fully formed nor completely validated. So you solicit feedback. You reach out to people you trust, and they make suggestions. You meet with potential business partners, and they make suggestions. You speak with prospective investors, and they make suggestions. And you continue this practice after you've raised money and you're up and running. Many of the suggestions sound reasonable. That isn't surprising. Most of the people providing you with feedback are intelligent and experienced. The problem, however, is that their feedback isn't consistent or cohesive. It's all over the map. And, if you do a Gilligan, and end up agreeing with everybody, you quickly end up overcommitted and strategically confused.

It may seem counterintuitive, but less really is more. If you want to build a great business, it's crucial to resist the temptation to spread yourself and the company too thin. Excellence demands focus.

PLANS ARE USELESS, PLANNING IS INDISPENSABLE

As my paternal grandfather, Howard Grossman, often (wryly) remarked, "It's difficult to predict . . . especially the future." He was reflecting on life in general, but his observation certainly applies to Silicon Valley.

No one in Silicon Valley has a crystal ball. Even the best-informed frequently make predictions that turn out to be misguided. For example, I recall a prediction that John Doerr made at a Kleiner Perkins CEO Summit in Aspen, Colorado, many years ago. The topic of discussion was a press release that Microsoft had recently issued. The company announced that it was expanding its authentication service – known as Microsoft Passport – to support universal single sign-on. With the new, improved Microsoft Passport, people would only need to log in once to securely access their applications, including those from companies other than Microsoft. The goal was to create an "internet trust network" with Microsoft at its epicenter.

Doerr abhorred this concept because he didn't want Microsoft to wield too much power over the internet. That wasn't a surprising perspective, especially given that he was one of the lead investors in Google. However, Doerr didn't merely express concern about Microsoft's grand new vision for Passport; he predicted that its long-term effect on both user privacy and security would be calamitous. At the time, I assumed that he was probably right. John Doerr was widely regarded as one of the top venture capitalists in Silicon Valley. He had a remarkable track record and had invested in many enormously successful companies, including Amazon, Intuit, Sun, and Symantec. He had as good or better access to information about technologically related opportunities and risks than anybody in the world. And he is a very smart guy. But in this instance, he was wrong. Although user privacy and security on the internet remain critical concerns, Passport's impact on them turned out to be relatively minor. It's difficult to predict, especially the future.

Through the years, I've made many erroneous predictions. At Inflection, I predicted we would go public in Australia. Wrong. At Tempo, I predicted we would sell the company to Mastercard. Wrong. At LiveCapital, I predicted we would revolutionize small business lending. Wrong again. The list goes on and on. And yet, I wouldn't say that I'm bad at making predictions. In fact, I think it's more a relative strength of mine than a relative weakness. Nonetheless, my predictions are frequently off base.

The main lesson I've learned about predictions is paradoxical. On the one hand, we have no business making them. On the other hand, our business depends on them. You need to make predictions to convince people to work for your company. You need to make predictions to convince people to invest. You need to be able to tell folks what you think will happen, or no one will follow you. Sometimes those predictions are based on data. Sometimes they're only based on hope. But either way, no matter how hard you try to accurately divine the future, you'll often miss the mark.

One of the main implications is that planning is impossible to do with any real precision. Plans are based on predictions. If you can't predict correctly, then you can't plan correctly. The consequence is that plans – however thoughtfully and rigorously conceived – become quickly outdated.

As a result, minimizing the effort devoted to planning can seem like a tempting path. Planning is time-consuming, particularly since plans need to be continually revised. Many early-stage CEOs, therefore, regard planning as an inconvenience and a waste of time. I don't agree with this perspective at all.

> **My view – to paraphrase Dwight D. Eisenhower – is that while "plans are useless, planning is indispensable."[13]**

The process of formulating a plan forces you to consciously prioritize, helping ensure that you and the team focus on the most critical activities. Employees also feel more motivated when they understand what everyone across the organization is working on and why. For both of these reasons – better focus and greater motivation – goals are more likely to be achieved when they've been explicitly defined, especially when the goals are tied to specific and quantifiable success metrics.

With that said, there is no question that plans need to be frequently modified. As former heavyweight champion Mike Tyson once famously observed, "Everyone has a plan until they get punched in the face."[14] Silicon Valley companies are metaphorically punched in the face all the time. So how do you stay on your feet? I've always believed in responding quickly but systematically. In every company that I've run, we've relied on a disciplined, quarterly approach to planning, with changes typically made every four to six weeks. Now and then, changes need to be made more frequently. While this type of process requires a relentless, ongoing commitment, the benefits far outweigh the costs. In the words of Eleanor Roosevelt: "It takes as much energy to wish as it does to plan."[15]

A LITTLE KNOWLEDGE IS A DANGEROUS THING

There is a quote from the movie *Wall Street*: "Life all comes down to a few moments."[16] The same can be said for business. At LiveCapital, one of those moments was at a board meeting where strategy was the main topic of discussion.

The prior 18 months had been exceptionally challenging. After the dot-com bubble burst in 2000, all hell had broken loose. We had been forced to discontinue our core product, introduce a new product that was only tangentially related, lay off most of the team, dramatically reduce our nonpersonnel costs, and recapitalize the company with new investors. It was a miracle that we survived.

Unfortunately, we weren't close to being out of the woods. Our new product, a trade credit management platform for large enterprises, had given us a new lease on life. We had signed several big customers in quick succession, which had enabled us to raise a new funding round. And yet, I felt uneasy.

Warning signs abounded. We had made substantial sales progress by closely collaborating with Dun & Bradstreet (D&B). However, D&B had recently replaced its CEO, and the new CEO appeared much less enthusiastic about working with us. Our sales pipeline, which had been rapidly growing, suddenly leveled off, and the cause didn't appear to be executional. We noted growing evidence that the enterprise software market was beginning to slump. In addition, we were struggling to implement the deals we had signed. Part of the challenge was that our product was new and still required considerable refinement. But more significantly, our new customers, all of them Fortune 500 companies, were extremely demanding and required a high level of customization.

My instincts told me that despite our recent sales success and funding round, we were in trouble. I became firmly convinced that we needed to pivot once again. And I had a specific approach in mind. The idea was to loosely model what we were doing on Salesforce.com, a company that, at the time, was relatively new. We would create a web-based solution for trade credit management that was extremely easy to use and highly configurable. Nothing like it existed. We would no longer build custom functionality. Furthermore, we would focus our marketing and sales efforts, not on large enterprises, but on midsized companies. We knew, based on our relationship with D&B, that D&B had a successful software business in the mid-market. But we also knew that D&B's product and underlying technology were awful. In other words, instead of continuing to partner with D&B, we would compete with them.

In advance of our board meeting, I presold this concept. I met individually with each of the directors and explained what I wanted to do and the reasons why. I also met with Bill Campbell, who, although he wasn't officially on the board, was in certain respects our most influential director. All of the conversations seemed to go smoothly. Coming into the meeting, it seemed that everyone was on the same page.

They were not – at least, not with me. I'm still not exactly sure what transpired behind the scenes. Presumably, after my meetings with the directors, there was a set of back-channel conversations to which I was not privy. All I know is that the board meeting ended up being an unmitigated disaster. When I presented the concept, absolutely no one supported me. The unanimous feedback was that we should stay the course and stick with our existing strategy. Even Bill Campbell, the most insightful businessperson I've ever met, disagreed with my recommended approach.

I don't recall what I stammered in response, but I do remember feeling astonished, confused, and betrayed. It was clearly not a vote of confidence in my leadership.

But the larger issue wasn't personal. It was that they were all 100 percent wrong. And I knew that they were 100 percent wrong.

> **The lesson that I would later reflect on is that people sometimes don't know what the hell they're talking about, and that includes people who are extremely intelligent and experienced.**

As a CEO, you live and breathe your business. You understand what is happening in an extraordinarily detailed and nuanced way. However, board members and advisors are far less knowledgeable about your company's specific situation. They're largely forced to rely on common sense and pattern recognition. What they know about your business primarily depends on what you share with them. And because they're busy people, they don't have very much time to process the information.

Board members and advisors are frequently insightful. They can add considerable value. Sometimes their relative distance from the company is beneficial because it helps them maintain objectivity and perspective. But there are times when their lack of understanding can become a major liability.

When the board meeting ended, I knew that I had done a terrible job. The problem wasn't that I was wrong, it was that I had been unconvincing. Despite my efforts to presell the concept, I hadn't made a sufficiently compelling case. I hadn't provided the board members or Bill with enough information, or at least enough of the right information, to correctly assess the situation.

Their knowledge was insufficient. They knew just enough to be dangerous, and it was my fault.

THE BUCK STOPS HERE

Shortly after the board meeting ended, I pulled the management team together to provide an update. Most of them hadn't attended the strategy discussion and were still in the dark.

Everyone was curious to hear how things had gone. The head of product management was the first to speak, asking, "What did they say?"

I shook my head and responded grimly, "They said no." I was still stunned by what had transpired, but was starting to regain my equilibrium.

A heavy silence followed. Then someone replied, "So what are we going to do?"

There was only one answer that I could give. "We're going to do it anyway."

It's unusual for a CEO and their board to be misaligned. Most issues are noncontroversial. And when issues are controversial, a consensus tends to rapidly form. Even when board members are skeptical about your point of view, you are generally given the benefit of the doubt. At other times, you read the room, decide the issue isn't worth fighting for, and quickly acquiesce.

But on rare occasions, the difference in perspective isn't easily reconciled. The two times that I've encountered this type of disconnect, the underlying dynamics have been similar. In both cases, I asserted that a new business model was urgently required. And in both cases, at least one board member strongly resisted because of their visceral attachment to the existing model.

In the LiveCapital example, we had just started working with three new venture capital firms. They had chosen to invest because they were enthusiastic about our large enterprise strategy and the big deals we had recently signed. Consequently, when only a few months later, I declared that our strategy needed a dramatic overhaul, their reaction was reflexively negative. They rejected what I was saying because it seemed too abrupt. They weren't emotionally ready to support a strategic pivot.

I next faced this issue 10 years later at a company named Attributor. It was my third tour of duty as a CEO. The original vision for Attributor was to enable media companies and publishers to efficiently detect online copyright infringement. But, despite raising $10 million, assembling an exceptionally talented engineering team, and building a highly innovative technology platform, the company struggled to generate much revenue. Eventually, with funds rapidly dwindling, co-founder and CEO Jim Pitkow proposed a last-ditch effort. He suggested diversifying the company's strategy by introducing a Facebook app focused on books. The idea was to compete with Goodreads, the largest website for readers and book recommendations.

A technologist at heart, Jim had earned a PhD in computer science, published extensively in technical journals, been granted a large number of patents, and provided technical assistance to a wide range of companies. But he was also an excellent salesman. First, Jim convinced existing investors to support his Facebook concept with additional money. One VC was particularly excited about the idea, and at the last moment, decided to provide an extra $1.2 million beyond the amount he originally planned to invest. Second, Jim persuaded the investors that he should be replaced as CEO by someone with business-to-consumer (B2C) experience. And third, he talked me into being his replacement.

I thought the Facebook concept was intriguing. But then I joined the company. It didn't take me long to realize that the idea was doomed. There were several insurmountable obstacles. We were understaffed and didn't have enough money to meaningfully expand the team. As a result, it wasn't possible to viably manage our legacy publisher-focused business and launch a new B2C business. Not only were the business models distinct, but the tech stacks were also incompatible. Moreover, we were bewildered about how to generate revenue with our new Facebook app, and worse, Facebook had no idea what to recommend.

I was displeased. To some extent, I felt that I had been sold a bill of goods. At the same time, I knew it was mainly my fault for not doing sufficient due diligence prior to joining. Yet, regardless of how I had gotten myself into the situation, it was now my problem to solve. So I went to the board, explained our quandary, and told them that the Facebook initiative needed to be discontinued. While no one was thrilled, most of the directors took the news in stride. But not the VC who had put in the incremental $1.2 million. He was furious.

I empathized with his frustration. His recent investment had been motivated by the Facebook opportunity. And now, just two months later, I was telling him that the Facebook project needed to be shut down.

However, he wasn't angry with Jim, the person who had convinced him to make the investment – he was angry with me. In a private discussion a few days after the board meeting, the VC vigorously expressed his displeasure. He told me, "You should be more like Steve Jobs. Where's the reality distortion? You need to figure out how to make this work. That's what you signed up for."

> **I thought it was the dumbest advice a board member had ever given me. I wasn't Steve Jobs, Jobs would almost certainly have agreed with my perspective if he understood the situation, and my role was to tell the truth, not distort reality.**

But I didn't say any of that. I decided instead to err on the side of civility. I acknowledged that we had different perspectives and left it at that.

Unfortunately, the VC was reacting emotionally rather than analytically. He had made a bad investment, but wasn't ready to feel accountable. It was too soon. He was looking for someone to blame because he didn't want to blame himself.

Shortly thereafter, I met with the management team, and someone asked the same question I had been asked a decade earlier at LiveCapital: "So what are we going to do?" And I gave the same answer. "We're going to do it anyway." We shut down the Facebook project the following day.

When you're the CEO, the buck stops with you. You need to make the decisions you think are right, regardless of whether they're popular or unpopular with your team or your board. While it's helpful to have alignment, and certainly more enjoyable, it's not the goal.

Of course, when you make decisions that people don't like, there can be unpleasant consequences. At SugarSync, for example, I wanted our new, recently promoted VP of engineering to modernize our technical architecture. But he resisted. He thought the effort would take too much time and too many resources. Unfortunately, I didn't see an alternative. If we retained our existing architecture, it was tantamount to giving up. So I kept pushing. Eventually, I shifted from suggesting to insisting. And at that point, he resigned.

Defying the board involves more personal peril. It increases the chance of getting fired. I suspect that a lot of CEOs agonize over that possibility. But it's not something that I've ever worried about myself. In my opinion, if you're a CEO and don't have the guts to do what you think is right, you should find a new line of work.

HERO BALL

The Suns, leading by two, were only 14 seconds away from extending the series to a seventh game. But the Bulls had the ball. The crowd thundered with desperate intensity – "Defense! Defense!" – as a closely guarded Michael Jordan dribbled up the floor. Everyone in the arena knew that He would take the final shot. After all, it was hero time.

But the unexpected happened instead. Jordan passed the ball forward, across the half-court line, to Scottie Pippen, who, instead of returning it to Jordan, swiftly whirled around and drove toward the hoop. Then, as he entered the key, he dished off to a cutting Horace Grant, who instantly fired the ball back out to John Paxson, who was standing alone behind the three-point line. Paxson didn't hesitate. In one fluid, confident motion, he planted his feet, rose into the air, and let it fly. From the moment he released the ball, the outcome was clear. And, when a second later, the ball passed through the net, the Bulls were (once again) world champions.

Over the course of his career, Michael Jordan won six championships. During his first six seasons, however, he didn't win any. While the quality of his play was consistently outstanding, his individual brilliance wasn't sufficient. Basketball is a team sport, and even the best players in history can't win championships by themselves.

Through the years, my perspective on the role of CEO has gradually but markedly shifted. In my first company, if I'm being completely frank, I regarded myself as the team's star player. I knew I wasn't the Silicon Valley equivalent of Michael Jordan, but I still believed my personal performance was the key to our success. Thus, whenever challenges emerged, I would immediately drop everything and get directly involved. In the words of another famous basketball icon, Larry Bird: "I wanted the ball in my hands for the last shot – not in anybody else's."[17]

But as I eventually came to learn, that isn't the job. When carried out most effectively, the role of CEO is devoted to coaching and general management. Your responsibility isn't to be the star; it's to assemble a team of stars, and then convince them to selflessly share the ball. To be sure, there are moments when you need to come off the bench and put yourself in the game. Sometimes you even need to take the last shot. But most of the time, your focus should be on game planning, drawing up plays, optimizing your roster, and motivating people to perform their best.

Playing hero ball as a CEO has many disadvantages. First, you're only one person, and there are only 24 hours in the day. No matter your aptitude or level of commitment, there is only so much you can individually accomplish. It takes a village to build a successful Silicon Valley company. Second, the more capable your team, the more likely your company is to flourish. But even if you succeed in hiring all-stars, you won't be able to retain them for very long if you're always hogging the ball. Talented people only stick around when they feel empowered. And third, as your company expands, the pace required to play hero ball becomes rapidly unsustainable.

> **Building a Silicon Valley company is like running a marathon rather than a sprint. It's a long-distance race and requires exceptional endurance. You need to learn to trust your team and delegate, or you're destined to burn out before you reach the finish line.**

Nonetheless, old habits die hard, and it can be tempting to reflexively go into hero mode any time problems arise. The temptation is especially strong if you don't have faith that your team will find a good solution without you leading the charge. But if you genuinely feel that way, and you're not just rationalizing your involvement, you have a bigger problem to address. You need to improve your team.

As a CEO, you need to know what's going on. Alignment with your team is vital when critical issues need to be resolved. But that doesn't mean you should always have the ball in your hands. In most cases, you're not meant to be the hero. You're meant to inspire other people to believe – to paraphrase Mariah Carey – that "a hero lies in them."[18]

BEGGARS MUST BE CHOOSERS

It's easy to recruit. There are always plenty of people looking for work. The hard part is recruiting people who are world-class.

I think this is the single biggest challenge that early-stage Silicon Valley companies face. It's a classic Catch-22. If you haven't made much progress, it's tough to convince great people to join. But if you don't have great people, it's extremely difficult to make much progress.

I've heard that a star engineer is five times more productive than an average engineer. I've also heard that a star engineer is 10 times more productive than an average engineer. I have no idea what the actual multiplier is, and I doubt that it's truly measurable with any accuracy. Nonetheless, I'm convinced that the number is large, and that it applies not only to engineering but to every other functional area as well.

We can observe similar dynamics in other industries. In the NBA, for example, stars are vastly superior to run-of-the-mill players. And more profoundly, they're the key to success. If you want to compete for championships, (multiple) stars are required. But getting them to join your team is easier said than done.

Recruiting stars in Silicon Valley is even harder. First, how do you identify who they are? In Silicon Valley, unlike the NBA and WNBA, you can't pull up stats and analytics to assess individual performance. There are no leaderboards that compare engineers or product managers to one another. Nor is there any way to know how someone performs without actually working with them first. I know that Steph Curry and Caitlin Clark are exceptional basketball players because I can go online and review their stats, or turn on the TV and watch them play. But in Silicon Valley, unless you've already worked with someone, the best you can do is make an educated guess about how good they might be. You can interview a job candidate, test their knowledge and personality, examine their resume, and check their references. You can meet with the candidate a second or even a third time. You can arrange for multiple people on your team to meet with the candidate, either individually or as a group. But in the end, no matter how rigorous your process, it's a gamble.

In the early days of LiveCapital, when I was relatively new to recruiting, my talent identification skills left a lot to be desired. If I thought someone was "good," my assessment proved accurate only about 20–30 percent of the time. Gradually, over the years, my hit rate improved. As my college roommate Brad Baker once observed, "You can't fall out of a cellar." I learned to take a more patient approach, ask more insightful questions, listen more closely, and pay greater attention to "hidden" nuances. Experience has its advantages. So now my hit rate is about 60–70 percent. In other words, I'm still wrong 30–40 percent of the time.

The second challenge is that most of the best people are already employed. By and large, they aren't the ones looking for jobs. From a recruiting standpoint, therefore, they effectively don't exist. In order to pursue them, you first need to know who they are. But unless you already know them, you have no way of targeting them.

And the third, and perhaps most notable challenge, is competition. Great people are hot commodities. Everyone wants to hire them, from innovative startups to IPO-ready unicorns to deep-pocketed behemoths like Google,

Apple, and Nvidia. To (loosely) paraphrase British race car commentator Will Buxton, "It's hard to win a gunfight with a spoon."[19]

Given all these obstacles, what is the best approach? The first step is easy: You contact the people in your personal network. If you know someone is talented and have a good relationship with them, you might be able to convince them to join. The people you know can also make valuable introductions.

Next, you boil the ocean. You post on job boards and your company website, leverage social media, implement an employee referral program, attend industry events, work with recruiting firms, etc. You do all the things that everybody else does, and hope – against all odds – to win the lottery.

Then, finally, you accept reality and start compromising and rationalizing. If your hiring standards are too high, you'll never hire anybody, and if your hiring standards are too low, you'll never hire anybody good. So you try to thread the needle. You assemble a team that you hope is good enough to get the company to the next level. And, if and when that proves successful, you progressively raise the bar.

Just like in the NBA and WNBA, it takes time to assemble a championship team. It doesn't happen overnight. But you get there a lot faster if your initial roster is strong enough to make the playoffs.

MIRROR, MIRROR ON THE WALL

Identifying great candidates and convincing them to join your company aren't the only obstacles when it comes to hiring. A lack of team alignment can also interfere.

In the early days of LiveCapital (then known as NetEarnings), we had a small but mighty two-person technology team: my father (Dave Grossman) and a friend of mine from high school (Jon Meyers). Dave has a background in advanced technology. He began his career as a high-energy physicist before joining IBM's Thomas J. Watson Research Center and transitioning to computer science. He then spent the next 25 years on the cutting edge, leading IBM's research into AI and robotics and contributing to a wide array of innovative activities. Meanwhile, Jon's background is in engineering. By the time he joined LiveCapital, he had worked for 10 years as a software developer at AOL, two Silicon Valley medical technology companies, and MIT Lincoln Laboratory.

The two men made a good team because each was strong where the other was relatively weak. Dave had far more management experience, but Jon had more experience in a production environment. Jon had better project-planning skills and cross-functional awareness, but Dave was more creative and moved faster. And, despite some minor, intermittent friction, the two generally got along well and collaborated effectively.

When it came to recruiting engineers, however, their philosophies weren't entirely in sync. Dave thought we should optimize for intellectual horsepower; Jon believed we should optimize for experience. They agreed on the profile of the ideal hire: someone who was an equal blend of world-class intelligence and world-class experience. Unfortunately, this type of "purple squirrel" was nearly impossible to find. After all, we were an unfunded, unproven, early-stage startup with big dreams and little reality.

Most of the job candidates that we initially attracted were either more brilliant than experienced, or more experienced than brilliant. Unsurprisingly, Dave preferred the former, while Jon preferred the latter. Further amplifying the lack of alignment, I had my own set of biases. The issue I was most preoccupied with was cultural fit. I wanted to make sure that the people we hired were collaborative, personable, trustworthy, and customer-centric. While Dave and Jon prioritized competence, I principally focused on personality. It wasn't that I didn't care about competence. Of course I did. And it wasn't that Dave and Jon didn't care about cultural fit. Of course they did. But all of us weighed these various factors differently.

> **Even in the best of circumstances, it's exceptionally difficult to recruit great people. But it's even harder when people disagree on the definition of "great." Moreover, such philosophical debates often have a heavy, high-context, visceral quality. They're not just superficial, tactical disputes; they're conflicts between competing values and belief systems. They're intensely personal, and so they're emotionally charged.**

Typically, people (at least implicitly) look to hire employees in their own image. I think of this as the "mirror, mirror on the wall" approach to team building. Our hiring preferences often reflect the personal attributes that we value the most in ourselves. It's not an ideal way to recruit, but it's understandable. And it reinforces the emotional subtext when folks have different perspectives on who to hire.

As a CEO, you frequently need to manage these types of situations, and it's always a delicate dance. In this specific case, if I sided with Dave, I might piss off Jon. If I sided with Jon, I might piss off Dave. If I vetoed too many candidates based on cultural fit (or more precisely, based on my personal definition of cultural fit), I might piss off both of them.

More profoundly, it wasn't obvious which approach was best.

> **Just because you're the CEO doesn't mean you know what to do. Many times, there isn't a "right" answer. There are only competing trade-offs and shades of gray. Nonetheless, an answer is required because when a lack of alignment is allowed to persist, dysfunction is the inevitable result.**

How do you determine the answer? One strategy is to trust your own judgment and unilaterally dictate the outcome. You have that authority as a CEO. And on occasion, it's the best solution. But it's usually better to forge (or at least try to forge) a consensus. People are happier when they feel like they've been heard and that their perspective is appreciated. A collaborative approach generally yields a more successful, more sustainable result.

In the end, Dave, Jon, and I all came to the same conclusion: We needed an approach that was pragmatic rather than religious. In other words, we needed to compromise. It was an obvious resolution, but "obvious" isn't always easy to implement.

REMOTE POSSIBILITIES

When I joined Inflection, my biggest apprehension was the team's geographic distribution. Despite employing only 200 people, we had offices in three different time zones (Redwood City, California; Omaha, Nebraska; Kyiv, Ukraine). The majority of our employees lived in Omaha, but most of our management team lived in Northern California. Of the 50 people who resided near Redwood City, more than half worked from home two to three days a week. The same was true of the 30 employees living in Kyiv. In addition, 10 people were fully remote. They lived in a wide array of locations, including Boise, Irvine, Raleigh, New York City, and Kharkiv, none of which were close to any of our three offices.

Several of my previous companies had offshore development teams, but none of them had more than one domestic office. Moreover, none of them had US-based employees who worked remotely. Inflection's geographic complexity was unlike anything I had experienced before. And that made me uneasy.

For one thing, I was worried about cultural cohesion. It's hard enough for an early-stage company to develop a healthy and unified culture in a single location. I assumed that with multiple locations, the challenge would be considerably greater. Sure enough, when I had the chance to visit Omaha and Kyiv for the first time, my concern was quickly validated. I liked the people I met, but it didn't feel like we were all working for the same company.

Each office was siloed from the others and culturally distinct. The vibe was different; the values were different. It didn't seem like a formula for success.

Also, relative to my prior experience, communication was more challenging. Meetings were difficult to coordinate due to time zone differences. Out of necessity, they were often (inconveniently) scheduled early in the morning or late at night. In addition, most meetings required us to use Zoom, which worked better for some topics than others. When cross-functional planning or group problem-solving was involved, in-person meetings were generally more effective, but they also required significant travel and expense. People on the engineering team, for example, needed to constantly shuttle between Redwood City and Kyiv. Moreover, ad hoc communication was severely limited, which made building relationships much harder. In previous companies, I would get to know people by walking around the office. I would pass someone in the hallway, see them in the kitchen, or stop by their desk and strike up a conversation. But this type of approach was rarely possible at Inflection. There were many days at Redwood City when more than 85 percent of the staff was located elsewhere.

The other problem was understanding the extent to which people were actually working. When everyone is in the same office, that's pretty easy to determine. You know people are working because you can see them working. But when folks are thousands of miles away or (ostensibly) working from home, a leap of faith is required.

And then COVID-19 hit.

Practically overnight, we were forced to go 100 percent remote. What happened next took me by surprise. First, the transition was fairly easy. We already had substantial experience with people working from home, and so we were able to rapidly adjust to the new reality. It was more of a struggle for some than others, but for most employees, the change was relatively straightforward.

Second, from a business standpoint, we didn't miss a beat. It became immediately apparent that my pre-pandemic concerns were unfounded. Not only did employees continue working hard from home, but they also worked longer hours because they didn't need to spend time commuting.

As for communication, we made an extra effort to ensure that information was actively shared and that everyone felt connected. Zoom and Slack became our lifelines. No, it wasn't perfect. There were too many meetings, and time zone challenges persisted. Getting to know people was difficult without any way to ever speak in person. Nonetheless, things operated well overall.

But the most significant impact was on hiring. When a company is fully remote, it doesn't matter where your employees live. They can literally be anywhere. The consequence is that you have vastly greater access to talent.

The numerical advantage is overwhelming. At Inflection, prior to COVID-19, our entire customer support team was located in Omaha. The company had selected Omaha (before I came on board as CEO) for good reason. The cost of living in Omaha is relatively low, and the city is well established as a hub for customer support. However, while there are many great people in Omaha, the total population is less than 500,000. The US population is more than 340 million. In other words, by recruiting nationally, we increased our pool of potential applicants by a factor of nearly 700. And, of course, recruiting internationally expanded the pool even further.

As with many epiphanies, the conclusion was obvious in retrospect. Inflection's geographic distribution wasn't a liability at all; it was an enormous strength. The issue wasn't that we had too much geographic diversity, but that we had far too little. Furthermore, from a cost perspective, we were wasting a lot of money on expensive offices that could have been spent in other ways.

> **My initial instincts were entirely wrong. Yes, there are challenges aplenty when it comes to effectively managing a remote, geographically distributed workforce. But the advantages far outweigh the disadvantages because of the quality of the people you can recruit.**

In recent years, some of America's most prominent CEOs, men like Andy Jassy, Jamie Dimon, Michael Dell, and Elon Musk, have come to a different conclusion. They've all mandated that employees return to the office full-time. Perhaps this type of "old-school" strategy is appropriate given the size and scale of their organizations. Perhaps it makes sense because their ability to hire great people is relatively unconstrained. Or maybe it's a mistake that reflects force of habit and a lack of imagination. I don't know.

Either way, I'm convinced that early-stage companies should fully and enthusiastically embrace a remote-first, geographically expansive approach. I learned this lesson by accident, and I'm very grateful that I did.

HOME IS WHERE THE HEART IS

Hiring is hard. Retention is even harder, especially when times get tough.

The more talented your team, the more likely the company will succeed. However, talented people are in constant demand. They don't need to work for you or your organization. They have a wide range of opportunities, and at any moment, can easily pick up and leave. One of your key priorities as a CEO is mitigating that risk.

Your ability to retain employees is heavily affected by the people you choose to hire in the first place. It comes back to the definition of what constitutes "great." If you only consider the quality of work that someone can do, you miss the bigger picture.

Different people have different motivations. One archetype is the "Soldier of Fortune," who regards employment purely (or primarily) through a transactional lens. For the Soldier of Fortune, job satisfaction depends on how they're rewarded. Tough-minded, self-interested, and dispassionate when it comes to their careers, they focus on practical considerations like making money, gaining experience, and getting promoted.

The alternative archetype – the "Dreamer" – is aspirationally and holistically inclined. They're human, and so they care about money and career, but what matters just as much to them are things like improving customers' lives, doing work they're proud of, being in an environment where they feel appreciated and supported, setting a high ethical bar, collaborating with people they like, and maintaining a healthy work-life balance.

> **All things being equal, it's far better to hire Dreamers than Soldiers of Fortune. The reason is simple. When adversity strikes, Soldiers of Fortune are the first to flee. The real warriors in a Silicon Valley company are the Dreamers.**

They're the colleagues you can count on in a crisis. When the bombs start figuratively falling from the sky, Dreamers are the only ones who will stand their ground and fight.

There is, however, an important caveat. Dreamers will only stick around if they feel deeply connected to the company. If you want them to fight for the company, they need to believe it's worth fighting for. And that isn't easily achieved. It requires you to demonstrate an unwavering commitment to all aspects of the employee experience. You need to not only espouse a set of aspirational values, but to build and maintain a culture that genuinely exemplifies those values.

Many Silicon Valley companies are explicit about the guiding principles they claim to follow. The terminology is generally similar across companies, with references to high-minded concepts such as integrity, respect, innovation, excellence, accountability, transparency, and teamwork. The words are compelling. But the reality seldom matches the rhetoric.

Generating a list of core values is easy. With the help of an AI tool like ChatGPT, the process takes less than a minute. Talking about your values is likewise easy. But talk is cheap. The hard part is operationalizing the values so they actually mean something.

There are two core challenges. One, you genuinely need to care about applying a values-based approach to running your business, or it won't happen.

> **I've interacted with many Silicon Valley CEOs over the years, and the truth is that values aren't top of mind for most of them. They may sometimes pontificate about the importance of values, but when they do, it's typically a performative, check-the-box exercise. In other words, it's bullshit.**

Their remarks are, at best, hollow – and at worse, disingenuous. Dreamers see through this type of CEO. They know when they're being spun.

Two, "walking the walk" in terms of company values requires steadfast, rigorous, ongoing dedication. It isn't easy. You need to embed the values, at a cellular level, into the operation of the business. In the hiring context, for example, it's critical that values be actively discussed with all job candidates. And candidates should be immediately disqualified when their values diverge meaningfully from the company's. Likewise, how well an employee embodies the company's values should have a substantial impact on their performance review. Also, every employee should be regularly surveyed on how well the company exemplifies its values, and the results should be transparently shared across the entire organization.

Operationalizing your values takes considerable time and effort. But if you don't, expect to ultimately pay a significant price. When adversity strikes, and it will, it's guaranteed, everyone – Soldiers of Fortune and Dreamers alike – will race for the door. You don't need Thanos to wipe out your team. You can do it all by yourself.

BEHOLD THE LORD HIGH EXECUTIONER (ACT 1)

When I was 9 or 10, my parents took my sister and me to an off-off-Broadway performance of Gilbert and Sullivan's musical *The Mikado.* I enjoyed it, or so I vaguely recall, but I don't remember many of the details. Thirty years later, my wife and I saw a film (*Topsy-Turvy*) that, with some dramatic license, tells the story of how *The Mikado* was created. It was only the second time that I had heard many of the songs.

The human brain works in mysterious ways. About two years after watching *Topsy-Turvy*, I had a dream relating to *The Mikado.* When I woke up in the morning, there was a song stuck in my head. It kept annoyingly repeating itself over and over, and the lyrics went like this: "Defer, defer, to the Lord High Executioner!"[20]

At first, I didn't know what to make of it. I knew it was an actual piece of music, and it sounded to me like Gilbert and Sullivan. But I couldn't figure out why that particular song would have spontaneously emerged from my subconscious. Then it occurred to me. The company I was running, LiveCapital, was on the verge of a major layoff. Our business fortunes had rapidly deteriorated, and we now needed to dramatically reduce our costs to have any hope of surviving. I knew what had to be done, but loathed the idea of doing it. Fifty people were about to have their lives turned upside down. And who was going to be the agent of this topsy-turvy disruption? It was me – the CEO – the company's Lord High Executioner.

I hate letting people go. Hate it, hate it, hate it, hate it, hate it, hate it, hate it. I hate it in the context of layoffs. I hate it in the context of poor performance. I even hate it in the context of misconduct. I hate everything about it. But there is no escaping it if you want to build a successful Silicon Valley company. After all, as aptly described by Hyman Roth (*Godfather II*), "This is the business we've chosen."[21]

Layoffs are particularly painful because the people directly affected are victims. They don't deserve to lose their jobs and have their lives severely disrupted. Their only mistake was being convinced to join your company. No, they aren't to blame – you are. Odds are high that the layoff is necessary because you hired too many people in the first place. It's an easy mistake to make, and often takes place in the immediate aftermath of a new funding round. You're feeling confident and finally have the money to accelerate your rate of progress. So you hire in anticipation of business results. And then business results disappoint.

There are exceptions, of course. Sometimes macroeconomic issues unexpectedly intrude. When COVID-19 emerged, for example, many companies immediately needed to downsize. Sometimes market dynamics rapidly evolve due to heightened competition, making reductions in force unavoidable. But usually, when early-stage companies need to lay people off, it's the downstream effect of overoptimism. It's the CEO's fault.

Regardless of who is to blame, however, it's your responsibility as CEO to fix the situation. And that requires burning the village to save the village.

Time is of the essence. The longer you wait, the more people you will have to lay off in the end. Hesitation and indecision are luxuries you can't afford. The situation is urgent and demands immediate action.

Intestinal fortitude is also required. You need to be bold and resist the temptation to cut too cautiously. Generally speaking, CEOs and other senior executives have a systemic bias when it comes to reducing headcount: an inclination to lay off too few rather than too many. The reason, in part, is that the task is so disagreeable and stressful that keeping people you can't afford is easy to rationalize. Moreover, it's difficult in the abstract to reimagine how a company will operate with a meaningfully smaller team. You worry that if you cut too deeply, you'll cause irreparable damage. As a result, you cut too little. And in the end, you do more damage rather than less.

I made this mistake at LiveCapital. We had grown to 125 people when it became apparent that layoffs were necessary. At the time, one of our board observers, an experienced venture capitalist from Kleiner Perkins named Doug Mackenzie, politely but ruthlessly asserted that we should cut the number all the way down to 30. His suggestion was based on pattern recognition rather than analysis. It didn't reflect a deep understanding of our strategy or team. He hadn't examined the specific consequences of taking such an aggressive approach. Nor did he have any idea how his recommendation would be implemented. Nonetheless, he thought that given our rate of spending, the amount of money we had left in the bank, and the business model challenges that we were trying to navigate, a team of 30 was probably sufficient.

I thought the recommendation was absurd and not at all helpful. I could sort of see how to run the company with only 75 people, but going below that number seemed like a recipe for disaster. Even a 40 percent reduction (from 125 to 75) would be operationally perilous.

Consequently, we went down to 75. As anticipated, it wasn't a pleasant experience. Agonizing, exhausting, and soul-crushing are the adjectives that come to mind. The transition was also very difficult from an operational perspective. Every aspect of the business was disrupted. Roles, responsibilities, processes, priorities, and timelines all needed to be substantially revised. It took six intense, tumultuous weeks for the situation to stabilize, whereupon I breathed a sigh of relief, and then had a jarring realization.

The company could be run with only 50 people. The 40 percent reduction should have been 60 percent. We hadn't been nearly as hard-nosed and courageous as I had fooled myself into believing. On the contrary, we had been conservative, way too conservative, and that created a serious dilemma. Quickly conducting a second round of layoffs seemed unthinkable. The impact on company morale would be devastating. Yet, not conducting additional layoffs would be irresponsible. Our monthly burn rate was more than $250,000 higher than it needed to be.

I wasn't sure what to do. Both options were appalling. It seemed to me that I needed to find some way to strike a balance. So, in the end, I decided to wait three months before implementing the additional reductions. Was that the right choice? I still don't know. I had cost the company $750,000, and morale had already taken a serious hit. But eventually things once again stabilized.

Unfortunately, despite best efforts, our business challenges persisted. Soon, the writing was on the wall. We needed to pivot and change our strategy. A key implication was that we were once again overstaffed. The appropriate number wasn't 50 people, it was 30. In other words, Doug Mackenzie had been right all along.

> **The lesson is clear. When you are forced to reduce head-count, don't trust your instincts. However many people you think you can let go, the actual amount is almost certainly higher.**

Counterintuitively, it's better to err on the high side than the low side. You want to do everything in your power to ensure that the layoff is a one-time event. As in movies, the sequel is always worse than the original.

Determining the size of a layoff is, thus, of vital significance. But it isn't the only consideration. Taking a thoughtful and sensitive approach to how the layoff is implemented is also an important priority. There are two key reasons. First, it's the right thing to do. The people losing their jobs are being put in a difficult position, and you're the one putting them there. To the extent you can help them, you should. Severance, for example, should be relatively "generous" (e.g., four to six weeks instead of two) despite the incremental cost. However, the second reason is even more critical. It's important to remember that there are two constituencies when you carry out a reduction in force: the people who are displaced, and the people who are retained. From a business standpoint, the latter group is far more important. If you want them to stick around – especially the Dreamers – you need to convince them that their faith in the company hasn't been misplaced. They will pay close attention to how their former colleagues have been treated, and will be anxious to hear your explanation for why a layoff was necessary. Above all, they will want to understand how you plan to turn the company around.

BEHOLD THE LORD HIGH EXECUTIONER (ACT 2)

It had never occurred to me that I might ever professionally join forces with my father (Dave). Then the stars unexpectedly aligned. Scott Belser and I urgently needed to find a technical co-founder, and Dave expressed enthusiastic interest. At the time, he was working for the USC Information Sciences Institute – having recently left IBM after 25 years – and was miserably unhappy in his new role.

The situation was admittedly unorthodox – sons don't usually manage their fathers. But the puzzle pieces fit, and so the three of us decided to defy convention and move forward together as a team. I'm profoundly grateful that we did.

In the context of my career, I've never had more fun or felt more joy than in those early years at LiveCapital with Scott and Dave. They were such an enormous pleasure to work with. That isn't to say that our business was rapidly thriving (it wasn't) or that we always knew what we were doing (we didn't). Nonetheless, it was the one and only time during my professional journey when work didn't feel like work. And as for my relationship with my dad, it couldn't have been better. Not only were we collaborating well, we were also connecting in a way that deeply resonated. I was enormously proud of him, and he was enormously proud of me – and that meant the world to both of us. It was a special and unforgettable experience.

Yet, regrettably, some gray clouds were visible on the horizon. To my surprise, despite his many years as a manager at IBM Research, Dave fit more naturally (and happily) into the role of individual contributor than senior leader. I hadn't anticipated this issue when we first started working together. Instead, I naively assumed that what he learned at IBM could be directly applied to LiveCapital. But the context was entirely different. At IBM, the people who reported to Dave were researchers devoted to trailblazing innovation. They weren't focused on launching products that would then be systematically and continuously improved over a period of months and years. Dave's management experience, therefore, didn't align well with the type of business that we were trying to build. Dave was accustomed to simultaneously leading multiple small teams, each working independently, as opposed to one large team that needed to be organized around a single, unified set of objectives. Moreover, the priorities at IBM Research and LiveCapital significantly diverged. At IBM Research, deadlines were less stringent – process optimization less relevant – and cross-functional alignment less important. What both Dave and I gradually came to realize was that he wasn't the right person to lead the technology organization into the future.

Consequently, as time progressed, it became increasingly difficult to define Dave's role. At first, we navigated this challenge fairly easily. Our team was still small, the management structure was still relatively informal, and the person who emerged as team leader (my high school friend, Jon Meyers) had developed a good working relationship with Dave when they had been the company's only two engineers.

Eventually, though, once we hired a new VP of engineering (Tim Fleming), the issue took center stage. For one thing, Tim and Dave were philosophically misaligned. Tim moved cautiously and methodically. Dave moved fast. The two styles were incompatible. As a result, neither was excited about working with the other. Moreover, Tim worried about Dave potentially undermining his authority and was very displeased that Dave was still on the company's executive team. Tim didn't like the feeling that anyone, least of all his boss's father, might be staring over his shoulder and second-guessing his decisions.

It was an uncomfortable and confusing situation. I'm reminded of a scene from *The Office*, where Michael Scott (played by Steve Carell) confesses, "I knew exactly what to do. But in a much more real sense, I had no idea what to do."[22] There wasn't an ideal solution, and so I did the best I could to thread the needle. Dave was effectively shifted to a "special projects" role that took advantage of his rapid programming skills. While he was still able to make a valuable contribution, he was no longer involved in the company's primary development work. Moreover, I reluctantly agreed to remove him from the executive team – to his understandable dismay.

But all of that was just a hint of what was yet to come. When, more than 18 months later, I needed to reduce our headcount from 50 to 30, I was forced to let Dave go. I didn't see an alternative path. We couldn't afford to have anyone focused only on special projects. Nor was there an obvious role he could play on the engineering team, even though by now Tim had left the organization. And, consequently, I thought that keeping Dave on the payroll would be a clear-cut case of nepotism. Not only would it damage my credibility with our remaining staff, but it wouldn't be consistent with my fiduciary duty.

So that's the way my father's career ended, "not with a bang but a whimper."[23] He had worked hard and done a consistently great job. And his reward was getting laid off by his son. It was deeply distressing for me, and a hundred times worse for him.

Do I regret what I did? Yes – and no. I think it was the right business decision. In fact, I think it was the necessary business decision. But it was a terribly hurtful thing to do. And my father deserved better.

BEHOLD THE LORD HIGH EXECUTIONER (ACT 3)

Over more than 30 years in Silicon Valley, I've seen many situations where a person is fired too slowly for poor performance. But I've never once seen a situation where a person is fired too quickly.

I've observed this dynamic in every company that I've run. Conflict avoidance isn't the only explanation, although it's certainly the most common. Most of us instinctively shy away from doing unpleasant things. And firing people for underperformance is exceptionally unpleasant. Regardless of how compassionately you try to deliver the message, the blow you are inflicting is deeply personal. You aren't merely criticizing the job that the employee has done; you're rejecting any possibility that their performance might meaningfully improve. It's a kick in the gut, and the news often generates tears, anger, or a combination of both. Even when someone responds stoically, their anguish is written on their face. Unsurprisingly, many managers (including CEOs) are inclined to stall when these situations arise.

Few people are willing to acknowledge that anxiety and a fear of confrontation are causing them to delay. They instead try to justify their hesitation with one of two common excuses. The first is that they haven't yet taken action because they hope the person's performance will soon get better. Unfortunately, hope isn't a strategy. When asked what gives them confidence that the employee's performance will suddenly and significantly improve, they have no answer. The second excuse is that they don't need to take action because they believe the employee will leave of their own accord. When asked when this will happen, they likewise have no answer. The reality, in both instances, is that they just don't want to deal with the issue. To put it bluntly, they're wimping out.

There is one other excuse that I've frequently heard that isn't based on conflict avoidance. Sometimes managers will say, "The employee is performing poorly, but I would rather have someone in that role than no one. If I fire them without a replacement already identified, our results will suffer." I was somewhat sympathetic to this argument earlier in my career. I don't feel that way any longer because it understates how much damage is caused by poor performance. When someone is doing a bad job, and you quickly move them out of the organization, there are two immediate benefits. First, it forces the team to creatively figure out how to fill the gap until someone new is hired. For a short period of time, some people need to step up and do additional work, but they usually don't mind, and the results almost always improve. In addition, strong performers are often quietly gratified when weak performers are removed. That may sound cold-blooded, but it's true. Strong performers have high standards, and they want those standards maintained. They generally have little patience for managers who drag their feet and tolerate ineptitude.

Foot-dragging is also common when the reason for termination is based on behavior rather than results. In the typical scenario, an employee is good at their job, but a nightmare to work with. They're arrogant, obnoxious, manipulative, untrustworthy, relentlessly negative, and/or constantly inciting conflict. But their performance is relatively strong. As a result, managers are often inclined to forgive – or at least rationalize – the bad behavior. And in my experience, that's rarely the right choice.

The problem with an employee like this – someone Bill Campbell would refer to as a "home-wrecker" – is the damage they inflict across the organization. Regardless of how skilled and capable they are, they adversely affect how the team functions and how well other people on the team perform. Even when their individual results are positive, their overall impact is almost always overwhelmingly negative. They are a corrosive force – a cultural cancer – and, in most cases, need to be urgently removed.

> **Firing people is a miserable part of the job, no matter how sound the rationale. In the companies that I've run, hundreds of people have been let go for either poor performance or toxic behavior, and it's just as painful every time. But if you want to build a great company, there is no alternative.**

THE BOARD IDENTITY

There is a well-known adage that "You can choose your friends, but not your family." For a Silicon Valley CEO, there is an analogous dynamic: You can choose your employees, but not always your board.

When you are recruited into a company as CEO, you inherit a board. You can decide not to join because of concerns about one or more board members, but you don't have the ability to replace them. Your authority regarding board composition is somewhere between limited and nonexistent.

As a founder/CEO, you have more control over this issue. For example, you can insist on diverse representation. But there are still practical constraints. Since you can't dictate who will invest in your company, you can't unilaterally determine who will sit on your board. You often need to compromise.

I've worked with approximately 25 different board members across the six Silicon Valley companies I've run. Most have been venture capitalists. Nearly all have added value, and in some cases, the value has been considerable. But there have been several notable exceptions.

At LiveCapital, for example, one of the board directors perpetually scrolled through his phone. He would spend at least 80 percent of every board meeting glued to his screen, compulsively checking and responding to messages. Now and then, he would lift his head, scan the room, and ask a question about something that we had finished discussing several minutes earlier. It was exasperating, and not only for me.

> **After one meeting, Bill Campbell took me aside and loudly exclaimed, "Mike, you need to slam your fist on the table and say, 'Stop looking at your goddamn phone! This is my fucking life, and you're gonna pay attention!'" Bill always made me laugh.**

At SugarSync, one of the board directors, a married man in his 60s, showed up to a meeting with a woman of about 30, whom he introduced as his "Ukrainian partner." I'm nearly certain that *partner* was a euphemism. The woman didn't speak much English and paid no apparent attention to what we were discussing. She devoted the first part of the meeting to carefully buffing her nails, which were long, evenly contoured, and coated in bright white polish. Then she spent the rest of the meeting scrolling through her iPad, her nails loudly clacking against the screen. As for the board member, he spoke more than he had at any previous meeting. He kept forcefully pontificating about topics that had very little to do with our business, all while repeatedly trying to catch the woman's eye. Unfortunately for him, she was preoccupied with her nails or iPad and didn't seem to notice. Our CFO (Peter Chantel) and I looked at each other several times and shook our heads in disbelief. The other board members seemed to share our bewilderment. Sometimes truth is stranger than fiction.

There have been other examples as well, although none quite as cinematic. In every instance, I've been reminded of a few fundamental truths. First, we all work for someone. You may be the CEO, but you still need to answer to your board. The cost of investment is a loss of control whether you like it or not. Second, board members aren't all created equal. Some are substantially better than others. And third, unless you think a board member is doing active harm, swallowing your frustration and going with the flow is usually the best approach. You want to pick your battles wisely because then it's easier to rally support when the outcome matters most.

THE TRUTH WILL OUT

When I joined SugarSync, the company was facing an existential crisis. Dropbox was eating our lunch, product development was moving at a glacial pace, sales were declining, and only six weeks of cash remained in the bank. We were running on fumes.

The team, however, with the exception of CFO Peter Chantel, seemed blissfully unaware. People, of course, understood that Dropbox was ahead of us and that we were falling farther and farther behind. But they didn't realize our situation was so dire. The general sentiment seemed to be that things were going OK, coming in second wasn't so bad, and we remained well positioned for long-term success.

Their optimism reflected what they had been told, or more precisely, what they had not been told. Good news had been shared while bad news had been withheld. I think I understand why my predecessor took this approach. She was simultaneously in denial and trying to emotionally protect the team and herself. Delivering bad news is a gut-wrenching experience for a CEO. Your employees, by and large, have fiercely devoted themselves to making the company successful. They've made considerable sacrifices, often working over weekends and late into the night. They've repeatedly demonstrated their loyalty and commitment, both to you personally and the company at large. Many aren't just your colleagues; they've become your friends.

These are people you want to help and support. The last thing you want to do is cause them pain. But when you stand in front of everybody and explain that the company is in trouble, pain is the unavoidable result. As you speak, a hush descends and the tension mounts. Anxiety rapidly ripples through the group. Some react with grim stoicism. Others look downcast, scared, or uncertain. Many turn away. Everyone is unnerved.

As a CEO, it's a terrible, empty feeling. You feel like you're letting everyone down. You feel like you're failing. You feel embarrassed. It sucks.

You also know that having shared this information, immediate, significant fallout is all but inevitable. The moment the meeting ends, many people will start looking for a new job, including people you can't afford to lose. It's inevitable. And that increases the likelihood of a death spiral.

As a result, there is a great temptation to sugarcoat the news for as long as possible. This is exactly what happened at SugarSync (pun intended). When you're running a company, and serious problems emerge, avoidance and spin can seem very appealing. Unfortunately, while this type of approach is easy to rationalize, it's never the right choice.

I say this for several reasons. The first is just a question of values.

> **Irrespective of business considerations, integrity matters. However uncomfortable it might be to tell the truth, telling the truth is better than spreading bullshit.**

Values aside, being honest with your team, both in good times and bad, is a smart business strategy. For one thing, problems are much easier to solve when they're openly discussed. When problems are swept under the rug, they don't magically disappear – they fester and intensify.

But the bigger issue is that when you lie to your team – and make no mistake about it, hiding the truth is lying – you sabotage yourself. Eventually, the truth will come out, and when it does, people will realize that they've been deceived, and you'll immediately lose all credibility. They'll never trust you again. The short-term impact is higher attrition. The long-term impact is irreparable damage to your professional reputation. For all of these reasons, when problems emerge, it's better to grit your teeth, stiffen your spine, and tell the truth.

During my second week at SugarSync, I heeded my own advice. I called the company together and shared what was really going on. I explained that our situation was precarious and that if we hoped to turn things around, urgent action was required. I told them (accurately) that our venture capital investors would provide additional funding before our money ran out as long as we quickly defined a concrete plan to cut costs, stabilize sales, and accelerate our development process. Then I opened the floor to questions and tried my best to answer them as authentically and directly as possible.

It wasn't an easy meeting. These types of meetings never are. For some, the news was a shock and deeply unsettling. For many, it primarily served to confirm their suspicions. I'm confident that many resumes were updated shortly after the meeting ended.

But it set us on the path to redemption. Although the team didn't yet know me very well, they at least knew that I was honest. I had established a foundation for trust, which was soon reinforced when, as promised, the VCs put in additional money.

Over the next several months, we were forced to make some difficult decisions. The company had spent the previous 18 months building out a freemium model. I quickly relegated that strategy to the dustbin of history. More painfully, we were forced to lay some people off, and several others chose to leave of their own accord. However, thankfully, we didn't lose any of the people we needed most.

The road ahead remained full of potholes, but at least we still had a car with a working engine.

THE GOOD NEWS ABOUT BAD NEWS

In the immortal words of Billy Joel, "Honesty is such a lonely word."[24] This sentiment often applies in Silicon Valley when things aren't going according to plan. The motivation isn't nefarious. It's just that no one wants to be the bearer of bad news.

My first day at Inflection coincided with the company's first quarter kick-off meeting. One by one, each member of the leadership team – about 30 people in all – presented to the rest of the group. Part of each presentation was dedicated to reviewing results from the prior quarter. And I quickly noticed a familiar pattern. If goals had been achieved, results were celebrated. But if goals hadn't been achieved, results were glossed over. In other words, good news was amplified, while bad news was minimized. Everything was sunshine and rainbows.

I'm reminded of an old joke. A doctor tells a patient, "I have some good news and some bad news." "I can't take any more bad news," the patient nervously responds. "Just give me the good news." And so the doctor replies, "We're naming this disease after you!"[25]

Avoiding bad news doesn't make it go away. Whatever problem is responsible for the bad news continues to persist. Voldemort doesn't magically disappear because people refuse to say his name.

Nonetheless, in my experience, most people are viscerally inclined to either sweep bad news under the rug or try to apply a positive spin. There are a variety of reasons. They don't want to get other people upset. They don't want to get other people in trouble. They don't want to be the messenger who ends up getting shot. They don't want to feel unsuccessful. They don't want to be held accountable. The latter two issues are usually the hardest to overcome.

Throughout my Silicon Valley career, I've relied on a systematic planning process. At the start of each quarter, goals – reflecting the company's key priorities – are defined in detail and shared with the team. Then, as the quarter progresses, the status of each goal is carefully monitored. And finally, at quarter-end, everyone gets together to review the results, which are color-coded as green, yellow, or red. Green means that the goal was achieved on time. Yellow means that it was achieved, but later than intended. And red means that it wasn't achieved.

It sounds simple. But it isn't, unless the result is green. When the result is – or is supposed to be – yellow or red, people often try to creatively "adjust" the rules of engagement so the news sounds good rather than bad. Sometimes they introduce different shades of green. For example, an achieved goal is color-coded emerald green, while a goal that has "almost" been achieved is color-coded lime green. Other times, they entirely disregard how the colors are meant to be applied. A goal is missed but is nonetheless classified as yellow rather than red because the team made some progress, and red doesn't "feel" like an appropriate assessment. Grade inflation doesn't only apply in an academic context, especially when people are being asked to grade themselves.

Of course, none of this is helpful. Moreover, it completely misses the point. Building a successful company depends on problem-solving. You can't solve problems if they're hidden or downplayed. And you can't solve them very well if they're not discussed in an open, honest, and direct way.

> **Consequently, one of your key priorities as a CEO is to create a culture in which people are comfortable sharing bad news. That requires dealing with issues constructively and maintaining your composure when things go awry. Accountability is critical, but that doesn't mean you need to be an asshole when goals aren't achieved.**

There are many reasons why a goal might end up yellow or red. Perhaps the goal was unrealistically ambitious. Perhaps priorities shifted in the middle of the quarter. Or perhaps the team didn't perform as well as hoped. But even if it's the team's "fault," solving the problem is much more important than assigning blame.

Old habits die hard, and so building this type of culture isn't easy. It takes time and effort to convince people that you can be trusted with bad news, and that you have the maturity not to overreact when results disappoint.

And, to that end, your mantra should be: "I want to know about bad news. I need to know about bad news. Bad news sucks. But it's good news when bad news is shared."

WHO'S THE BOSS?

You have the authority as a CEO to tell employees what you want them to do. Most of the time, they nod their heads and do what you want. Sometimes they push back and recommend an alternative approach. If they convince you that they're right, you agree to follow their lead. If they don't convince you, you thank them for the feedback, explain why you disagree, and reiterate your original request. And then, even if they're still not entirely aligned with your perspective, they nod their heads and do what you want.

On occasion, however, when you tell employees what you want them to do, they respond with passive-aggressive defiance. They nod their heads and then refuse to do what you want. These types of situations are deeply dysfunctional, exceptionally frustrating, and can be very difficult to manage. I'll provide two specific examples.

My fifth company, named Zetta, specialized in cloud-based backup and disaster recovery. It was the only organization I've run where advanced, patented technology was the core competitive advantage. Zetta was the first company to develop technology that enabled enterprises to back up and recover large datasets over the internet without the use of hardware appliances.

I was brought on as CEO in a last-ditch effort to revitalize the company's fortunes. Zetta had been founded seven years earlier, and despite its impressive technical foundation, it was losing money and struggling to grow revenue. Product-market fit had still not been fully achieved. There didn't seem to be a viable way to strategically pivot. And one of the company's co-founders had recently decided to leave, which both reflected and amplified the team's low morale. It was, to say the least, a very challenging situation.

The company required a turnaround on multiple fronts. Sales and marketing leadership needed to be promptly replaced and upgraded. Costs needed to be substantially reduced. Morale needed to be urgently improved. This latter issue was the trickiest to remedy because the team seemed so jaded, listless, and gloomy. I had never experienced a vibe as negative as this in any of my previous jobs. When I first visited, the office environment made me think of a sensory deprivation tank. The space was only dimly illuminated because some engineers inexplicably preferred to keep the lights off. It was also exceptionally quiet. People worked silently in their cubicles and seldom interacted. When my friend and frequent collaborator, Peter Chantel, joined the company as CFO the following week, he immediately began referring to the office as "the tomb."

One of my top priorities was fostering better communication across the team. To that end, I introduced a weekly all-hands meeting. It was an opportunity for people in each department to learn about what was happening in other departments. Most of the updates were informal, but every week I asked one of the company executives to prepare and deliver a short presentation, around 15 to 20 minutes in length.

Several months after joining the company, I approached one of our engineering leaders about providing a high-level overview of our technical architecture. He casually responded, "Yeah, that sounds good," and we agreed that he would present the following week. Then, the following week, about two hours before he was scheduled to speak, he stopped by my desk and said that he hadn't had time to complete the slides. I replied, "No problem. How about next week instead?" He agreed. Then a week later, the same thing happened. About two hours before the meeting, he stopped by and said he needed additional time. I gave him another one-week extension. Then the same thing happened again the following week.

This time, I asked him what was going on. Was he reluctant to present, and if so, why? He dismissed my concern: "No. It's not a problem at all. I've just been busy." While I wasn't satisfied with this response, I decided not to press the issue any further. I offered a two-week extension and he readily agreed. Then, sure enough, two weeks later, he again told me that he wasn't ready. It was at this point that I started to realize two things. First, he would never be ready. He wasn't merely busy; he was intentionally defying the request. And second, he was angry with me for having made the request, and that anger was reflected in the fact that he had never once apologized for failing to deliver.

I still don't understand what the issue was. Was he nervous about public speaking? Was he confused about what information to include in the slides? Did he think that describing the company's technical architecture to nonengineers would be a waste of time? Was he disgruntled about how hard he was working and expressing frustration in a dysfunctional way? I have no idea. But whatever the motivation, he wasn't going to do it. And that left me with two choices: drop the request or fire him.

From an emotional standpoint, I couldn't wait to fire him. Not only did I think he was behaving unreasonably, but I felt personally disrespected. The more I thought about the situation, the more infuriated I became. From a practical standpoint, however, I knew that firing him would be a mistake. He was good at his job and would be difficult to replace. Consequently, the decision was easy. I swallowed my ego and let him off the hook. I told him, "It's obvious that you're very busy. Let's not worry about the presentation for a while." He said, "OK." And we never talked about the issue again.

I first experienced an employee's passive-aggressive defiance 15 years earlier, when I was running LiveCapital. At the time, the company was actively promoting its small business lending marketplace. We were spending an enormous amount of money on marketing, and our largest expense was a $4 million advertising deal with Yahoo. When we signed the deal, we were very bullish about the positive impact it would have on our business. Six months later, however, we were much less hopeful. The ads generated minimal revenue despite diligent efforts to optimize the results.

I lamented having committed so much money to Yahoo and expressed that view to the business development executive responsible for managing the relationship. She disagreed. Her perspective was that the brand value of being associated with Yahoo was significant, and that our ROI analysis understated the benefit we were deriving. She also thought it was vital to maintain the relationship with Yahoo because competition in our space was heating up. I was deeply skeptical. I told her that although I respected her opinion, I didn't agree with it, and that barring a sudden improvement in ad conversion, I planned for us to stop working with Yahoo in the not-too-distant future.

Two weeks later – unbeknownst to me, our CFO (George Northup), and everyone else in the company – the business development executive signed an addendum with Yahoo obligating us to spend an incremental $500,000. About two weeks after that, we received a bill from Yahoo for this amount. George immediately rushed over to my desk and asked, "What the hell is this?" And of course, I had no answer.

I then hurried over to the executive and asked if she knew anything about it. She looked back at me with guilty dismay, hesitated for a moment, blanched, turned red, looked like she was starting to hyperventilate, and then responded, "Yes, I agreed that we would spend an additional $500,000." I asked, "Verbally or in writing?" She answered, "In writing. They sent over a contract, and I signed it," to which I replied, "But why would you do that? You weren't authorized to do that. You know I didn't want to spend any more money with Yahoo." This time, she didn't respond.

We sat in awkward silence for the next minute or so. I was flabbergasted and didn't know what to say. I'm not sure what she was thinking, but she likewise kept quiet. And then finally, she said, "I'll pack up my stuff and leave." I made no effort to dissuade her.

> **CEOs have a lot of influence, but not a lot of power. The job depends much more on persuading people than commanding them.**

You can tell employees, in no uncertain terms, what you want them to do, and most will usually comply. But there are many exceptions. Sometimes people will leave. Sometimes people will defy. In the real world, the CEO isn't always the boss.

On a final note, we refused to pay Yahoo the incremental $500,000. They threatened to sue, but we called their bluff. That $500,000 would later save the company from oblivion.

THE ILLUSION OF GOOD

When I started at SugarSync, one of the first people I met with was the VP of marketing. I shared a little about my background, learned a bit about his, and then asked some questions about his department. I wanted to better understand what the marketing team was working on, and how well (or poorly) he thought things were progressing. He seemed excited to tell me. He leaned forward, flashed a self-assured smile, and proudly declared, "We've had an extremely successful year. I think we've done a really good job." That certainly sounded promising, so I nodded in support and said, "Great. Tell me more." He paused, perhaps for dramatic effect, then continued.

"A year ago, we had almost no free users. Now we have more than five million."

I was much less impressed by this statistic than he was clearly hoping. I'm sure that I visibly winced before asking my next question: "How many have converted from free to paying?" His reply, which was immediate, forceful, and defensive – "That wasn't the objective!" – impressed me even less. For the next several seconds, we silently contemplated each other. And then I finally responded. "I don't understand. Does that mean that the conversion rate is unusually low? Isn't the purpose of having a freemium model to generate paying customers? Otherwise, what's the point?" His answer, which entirely avoided my question about conversion rate, didn't inspire much confidence. "Well, I suppose eventually. But that hasn't been the focus." I was only able to get specific details about the (near-zero) conversion rate after he resigned the following week.

I doubt that the VP was being disingenuous. He seemed to honestly believe that he was doing a good job, and my less-than-enthusiastic reaction didn't alter his perspective. He quit because he could see the writing on the wall with me as a boss, not because he thought he had done anything wrong. I'm confident that today, many years later, he still thinks that it was a job well done.

One of the most significant challenges in running a Silicon Valley company is that employees often have an overly high opinion of their own performance. I'm reminded of Garrison Keillor's fictional town of Lake Wobegon, a place where "all the women are strong, all the men are good-looking, and all the children are above average."[26]

> **In Silicon Valley, as in Lake Wobegon, people tend to overestimate their own abilities in relation to others. They're convinced that they're doing a good job because they desperately want to believe it – and because they convince themselves that working hard equates to good performance. But they often don't have a frame of reference for what truly qualifies as "good."**

I've found this to be a particularly challenging issue in the engineering context. When technical issues are discussed, it's relatively hard for me as a nonengineer to verify what I'm told. And through the years, what I've been told has often amounted to nonsense.

Since becoming a CEO, I've worked with 15 different VPs of engineering, and I've asked every one of them the same question: "How good is our technical architecture?" With few exceptions, the answer has always been identical: "Very good." Moreover, each exception shared an identical profile: They began their tenure after the architecture was already in place. In other words, when it comes to technical architecture, every VP of engineering likes their own brand.

Regrettably, many of the "very good" architectures were, in fact, not very good. How did I figure out that I had been misinformed? With difficulty. As I gained experience, I became better at recognizing the symptoms of poor architectural design (e.g., quality problems, scalability issues, slow development cycles). And I began insisting that outside experts be brought in to provide an independent assessment.

Of course, as a CEO, you're also susceptible to the illusion of good. You want to believe that you're doing a good job, and you want to believe that the people on your team are as well. But wanting something doesn't make it true. So how do you know? Unfortunately, you often don't. The best you can do is surround yourself with people – on your board and management team – who are highly experienced, have a track record of excellence, and will tell you when things need to be improved.

Early in my career, I was convinced that the value of experience was overrated. I believed that as long as you were smart, adaptable, and determined, you could figure anything out. I still (largely) believe that to be true. Unless you're an engineer for SpaceX, what we do in Silicon Valley isn't rocket science. But it's a lot easier to get from point A to point B if you already know the way. If you want to correctly identify "good," it helps to have seen it before.

THE ILLUSION OF SPEED

Time works differently in Silicon Valley. Everything is geared for speed. If Silicon Valley had a patron saint, it might be famous, fictional race car driver Ricky Bobby from *Talladega Nights* – the man with the mantra, "I wanna go fast."[27]

The need for speed has a variety of underlying causes. It's partly a result of competitive urgency. If you don't move fast, someone else might move faster, causing you to miss out on the opportunity. It's partly a function of financial constraints. If you don't move fast, you'll run out of money without having made enough progress to raise additional funds. It's also partly the consequence of working in an industry that attracts pathologically impatient people. And all of these factors are mutually reinforcing.

So when it comes to Silicon Valley, speed is the name of the game. However, trying to go fast isn't the same thing as actually going fast. In fact, counterintuitively, the opposite result is often achieved. The most famous historical example is the *Titanic*. In an effort to cross the North Atlantic quickly, the ship's speed was maintained despite multiple warnings about drifting ice. It seemed to be an effective strategy for the first three days. Then, on the fourth day, the ship struck an iceberg and sank to the bottom of the ocean. "Move fast and break things," the philosophy advocated 100 years later by Mark Zuckerberg, doesn't always produce a good outcome. Sometimes what gets broken is unfixable.

In Silicon Valley, this issue usually plays itself out in a more insidious way. Many early-stage firms become obsessed with rapid feature development. They develop a culture focused on relentlessly pumping out new user-facing functionality. Often, this kind of tactical, whirlwind approach is initially successful. Customer adoption is accelerated, which serves to reinforce the obsession. But there is a considerable downside. In their haste, these companies tend to constantly cut corners. They don't spend much time on technology architecture or design. They don't spend much time ensuring that their code is well written. And when these issues are persistently neglected, major problems invariably arise.

Before long, the technology platform becomes a chaotic and tangled mess – what is commonly referred to as "spaghetti code." The Winchester Mystery House is the metaphor I prefer to use. A bizarre, maze-like mansion in San Jose, California, the Winchester Mystery House has been a tourist attraction (or more precisely, a tourist trap) for more than a century. Once the home of Sarah Winchester, heiress to the Winchester gun fortune, the house reflects 36 years of rapid, random, impulsive, and incoherent design. Hundreds of rooms and thousands of doors and windows were built, without any master plan. Sometimes features were constructed and then immediately hidden or destroyed. A seven-story tower was repeatedly razed and rebuilt, 16 separate times. There are partly completed staircases with no destination, doors and windows that open onto brick walls, and chimneys that reach only partway to the ceiling. None of it makes any sense.

Silicon Valley companies that build Winchester Mystery House–like technology platforms pay a heavy price. First, quality suffers. Things begin breaking all the time, which causes customer satisfaction to severely decline. Identifying the root cause when something breaks is often elusive. And when you finally figure out the issue and try to fix it, other things immediately break.

But the most significant issue relates to speed. Silicon Valley companies that figuratively live in the Winchester Mystery House become immobilized. They lose the ability to move fast. And once it's lost, it's practically impossible to get back.

> **So whenever I see people who pride themselves on speed, I've learned to respond with caution. Often what they think is speed is only an illusion. It's fun while it lasts, but it doesn't last long.**

Relentless velocity is absolutely a key priority. But achieving it, ironically, depends on patience and planning. In other words, if you want to move fast, you sometimes need to slow down.

THE SPEED DEMON AND THE CONSULTANT

An inherent (arguably healthy) tension exists between speed and analysis. Go too fast and you go in the wrong direction. Analyze too much and you don't go anywhere. It's best to maintain a balance between these priorities. But balancing speed and analysis is hard because people's personalities get in the way. Some folks (the "Speed Demons") have a bias for speed. Instead of "ready-aim-fire," they prefer "ready-fire-aim" and feel ill at ease and frustrated unless action is being taken. Others (the "Consultants") have a bias for analysis and like to rigorously examine and reexamine issues before action is taken. Their "ready-aim-aim-aim" approach tends to get them stuck.

One of the biggest Speed Demons I've ever met, Ryan Velez, was leading customer support when I took charge of Inflection. Ryan is an unstoppable force – a whirlwind of relentless drive, restless energy, and perpetual motion. And he delivers remarkably rapid results. If you have a mission-critical, time-sensitive, operational project with multiple moving pieces – such as standing up a call center – Ryan is your man. He is extremely well suited to working in companies growing at a blistering pace, at which major new projects are continuously being launched.

Ryan loves building new things – fast. It's what motivates him. He is, however, far less interested in optimizing things that have already been built. And this is the problem that emerged shortly after I joined Inflection.

Ryan was just completing a large project, the opening of a new call center in Omaha, Nebraska. But there were no other comparable projects in the pipeline. Part of our business was growing, but other parts were shrinking, and one of the key operational priorities was carefully managing that transition. Furthermore, in the part of the business that was growing, systems and processes needed to be significantly refined. They had been cobbled together in a hurry, and improvements were now required. Ryan's role was evolving. The situation demanded that he recalibrate his approach from "ready-fire-aim" to "ready-aim-fire."

I had only been CEO for about six months when Ryan abruptly decided to leave the company. I don't believe that my increased emphasis on analytical rigor was the driving force behind his departure. His primary motivation appeared to be financial. Nonetheless, I think the shifting nature of his role was a contributing factor. The need for him to be more of a Consultant and less of a Speed Demon didn't seem to resonate.

Several months later, I hired Stan Denker as Ryan's replacement. Stan was, quite literally, a consultant. While he had some experience as a customer support leader, he had spent most of his career advising companies on operational performance. Ryan was actually the person who recommended Stan.

Stan is one of the most capable Consultants I've ever worked with. He is analytically creative and intellectually rigorous. He loves examining data and tenaciously looking for insights never before revealed. However, Stan is less comfortable operationalizing those insights. Naturally cautious and risk-averse, he prefers to keep studying issues until the conclusions are irrefutable. As a result, relatively minimal progress is made.

In the end, things didn't work out with Stan. Going too fast in Silicon Valley can create problems, but going too slow is worse. It was around this time that Ryan unexpectedly reached out. He was back on the job market and expressed regret for having ever left Inflection. With some trepidation, I decided to bring him back.

I should have known better. Things had evolved considerably since Ryan's departure. When he left the company, all our customer support reps worked in close physical proximity, in a single office in Omaha. By the time he returned, everyone was working from home. Reps were geographically distributed all around the country, and the team had nearly tripled in size. Thus, the management challenge had become far more complex. The potential for misalignment had sharply increased, so changes needed to be made more carefully. Nonetheless, many changes were urgently required. The situation ideally called for a customer support leader who was an equal mix of Speed Demon and Consultant. But that wasn't Ryan. He would either frustrate me by charging ahead without sufficiently considering the consequences, or I would frustrate him by holding him back. We both realized, fairly quickly, that it wasn't a match made in heaven.

Managing the tension between speed and analysis is never easy because, as the saying goes, "A leopard never changes its spots." The bias toward speed or analysis is deeply ingrained, almost pathologically so. You can't force a balance where none exists. It never works. You can convince a Speed Demon to take a little more time or inspire a Consultant to move marginally faster, but in the end, they are who they are. And if that's a problem, they're not to blame. The fault lies with you and your company for hiring them in the first place.

I've come to believe that, in a perfect world, an expedited version of "ready-aim-fire" is usually the best approach – let's say 50–70 percent Speed Demon and 30–50 percent Consultant. But many people aren't wired that way, and that creates two practical challenges. The first is determining what mix of speed and analysis is acceptable for each position you are looking to fill. The second is establishing a recruiting process that enables you to accurately assess whether job candidates fit that profile before hiring them.

I've struggled with the latter challenge in particular. And I think I know why. At the end of the day, for better and worse, I'm more Speed Demon than Consultant. The issue doesn't only apply to the people on your team.

GENERAL SPECIFICITY

Let's say you want to build a house and sell it immediately for maximum value. In the best-case scenario, you know in advance exactly how the house should be designed. You've figured out that it should be a raised ranch made of pine, with exterior siding made of stone, that's 25 feet tall, and has four bedrooms, two bathrooms, and a garage. So you build a house with precisely those specifications. Then you put the house on the market and sell it the next day for a huge profit. In the words of Sacha Baron Cohen, "Great success!"[28]

But what if you only *thought* you knew how the house should be designed, when in reality, you didn't understand what people were actually looking for? What would happen if you built the house described above, only to discover that folks actually want one level, 15 feet tall, made of spruce with exterior siding made of brick, and three bedrooms, 1.5 bathrooms, and no garage? You wouldn't be able to magically transform the house you've built into the house people want to buy. Consequently, your options would be limited. You could either knock the house down and build a new house in its place, or sell the house you built for pennies on the dollar.

Alternatively, let's say that you want to build a house but have literally no idea how it should be designed. You aren't sure whether it should have one level, two levels, or 35. You aren't certain if it should have three bedrooms and two bathrooms, or 47 and 11. Maybe it should be made of spruce, but maybe stainless steel would be more appealing. Perhaps it should have an onion-shaped dome, or an observation deck that slowly rotates for 15 minutes, in a counter-clockwise direction, at noon each year on the summer solstice. Who knows?

Moreover, you've borrowed money to finance construction, so you need to start building relatively soon. After all, the clock is ticking. But you're worried that because you don't fully understand the requirements, you'll build the house the wrong way – and then no one will want to buy it. As a result, you optimize your design for modularity. You embrace a Lego-like approach. The house initially looks like a raised ranch, but you leave open the possibility of adding an onion-shaped dome or a rotating observation deck later. You use wood for the frame, but make it possible to substitute stainless steel. And so on. In the end, your "Lego" house provides enormous flexibility, but the amount of time and money required to design and build the house is exponentially greater.

This type of tradeoff – between the specific and the general – is inherent to software development. The more specific the design, the faster you can initially move, but the less flexibility you'll have to make changes and enhancements in response to evolving customer needs. The more general – and extensible – the design, the more optionality you create. But if a design is overly general, then you spin your wheels defining and building capabilities that aren't actually required. And in the process, your pace of development slows to a crawl.

When I first became a CEO, I was laser-focused on what we were building. However, I paid too little attention to how it should be built.

> **One of the main lessons that I've learned through the years is that the "how" matters almost as much as the "what."**

And getting the "how" right depends on balancing the specific and the general.

A FOOL FOR A CLIENT

Although I ended up pursuing a career in business, I went to law school rather than business school. I spent two summers working at large corporate law firms in Melbourne and San Francisco, gaining hands-on experience in legal research, client communication, and contract drafting. I was also admitted to the bar in both New Jersey and the District of Columbia. So I'm a lawyer – sort of. Except for my two summer jobs, I've never practiced law. I never developed much in the way of practical legal expertise, and most of what I learned, I've long since forgotten. In other words, when it comes to law, I know just enough to be dangerous. And on one occasion, that nearly led to disaster.

I was running LiveCapital at the time. We were in the midst of our fifth strategic pivot in seven years. The company's original concept had been to create the first online, one-stop shop for small business financial services. Then we narrowed our focus to lending and created the first online marketplace for small business loans. Then we redirected our attention to enabling banks to offer small business loans through their websites. Then we moved away from loans entirely, developed a trade credit management platform for large enterprises, and partnered with D&B. And now, we were shifting away from large enterprises and toward the middle market. We had built the first cloud-based software platform for trade credit management, terminated our agreement with D&B, and negotiated a strategic alliance with Experian, D&B's leading rival. The next step was finalizing the contract with Experian.

Our company was financially stable, but we nonetheless needed to tightly manage expenses. Some years earlier, we had raised more than $50 million (for business model #2), but most of that money had long since been spent. If, in the immortal words of Cher, "I could turn back time,"[29] I would have substantially reduced our costs much earlier. But hindsight is 20/20. The best I could do was enforce a more cautious approach moving forward. It was necessary, therefore, to restrict all types of expenditure, including legal fees.

The contract draft Experian sent us wasn't particularly complicated or nuanced. It was a standard distribution agreement, only six pages in length. Since Experian wasn't investing in LiveCapital, and the relationship between the two companies wasn't meant to be exclusive, there wasn't much to negotiate. They had included a sentence that would provide Experian with a modest level of preference, but the language seemed unobjectionable to me. While I briefly thought about asking our outside counsel to review the document, it seemed like an unnecessary expense. After all, I was a lawyer myself. I might not be an expert in contract law, but this agreement didn't require an expert's involvement. I signed the contract several days later.

Our new solution started immediately gaining traction. The only competitive mid-market product for trade credit management was sold by D&B and was out of date, inflexible, and difficult to use. Many of our early adopters had been frustrated for many years with D&B's offering. Meanwhile, the relationship with Experian had gotten off to a slow start but seemed to be moving in the right direction. They were certainly delighted by the progress we were making at D&B's expense, and as a result, had intensified their efforts to help us accelerate sales.

It was at this point that D&B reached out to us and expressed strategic interest. They too had noticed the progress we were making at their expense. And more profoundly, they had concluded that quickly and dramatically improving their technical capabilities was a strategic imperative. They were intrigued by the product and platform we had built, but what most interested them was our technology team.

Discussions rapidly progressed. I would have loved to create a bidding war between D&B and Experian, but I knew that, unfortunately, Experian wouldn't engage. The Experian division we were dealing with (Business Information Services) was, for various reasons, not in a position to acquire us.

Everything appeared to be on track. With due diligence looming, we began scrambling to consolidate all our documents for efficient review. As part of this effort, I decided to carefully reread each of our (many) contracts just to ensure that we didn't have any unidentified risks. This activity was exceptionally tedious and time-consuming, and reminded me why I had chosen to pursue a career in business rather than law. Some people may enjoy slogging their way through dozens of contracts, one after the next, for the better part of a week, but I'm most definitely not one of them. The only consolation was that, after several dreary, mind-numbing days, I was nearly finished and hadn't found anything of significance. It was late on the third day when I finally got to the Experian agreement.

The first time I reread the sentence about preference, I had a vague sense that something wasn't quite right. The language was different from what I had remembered. There was something disconcerting about the way it was written, but I couldn't initially figure out what it was. So I read it again. And then, with mounting horror, I read it a third time. All of a sudden, I felt sick to my stomach. How could I have been so stupid? The sentence could reasonably be interpreted in two entirely different ways. The first way – my original interpretation – was harmless. But the alternative interpretation was potentially devastating. Read the second way, the language would prevent us from being acquired without Experian's prior approval.

I urgently scheduled a board call for the following day. The feedback I received was far more encouraging than I had anticipated. All the directors thought my original interpretation reflected the plain meaning of the language, and that, consequently, the risk wasn't very high. They recommended that I say nothing and do nothing about it, and wait to see if D&B expressed any concern.

However, later in the day, I spoke to Bill Campbell, who, to put it mildly, had a different response. Bill sharply exhaled, muttered under his breath, and then declared something to the following effect: "Fuck. Fuck. Holy fuck. Your board doesn't know what the hell it's talking about. What are they thinking? This is absolutely going to kill the deal. Of course D&B will notice." Then he suggested a solution. He told me that I should meet in person, in Orange County, as soon as possible, with my senior contact at Experian (Mark Zablan, president of Experian Business Information Services), explain the situation – without identifying the prospective buyer – and ask that he let us out of the agreement.

My initial reaction was disbelief. I said, "Bill, how am I supposed to convince him to do that?" But Bill was undeterred. He said, "I know this is a Hail Mary. That's what the situation demands. You tell him the truth – that getting acquired would mean a lot to you and the other people on your team. And you tell him that you would really appreciate his help. Maybe he'll say yes. At this point, you have nothing to lose."

I decided to listen to Bill. It was a good decision. Mark Zablan was extremely gracious and agreed to my request. A week later, our relationship with Experian was formally terminated. And then a few days after that, D&B notified me about a "showstopper" they had identified in our contract with Experian. Thankfully, I was able to tell them that the problem had already been resolved. The deal with D&B closed shortly thereafter.

It sometimes makes sense to cut corners when trying to save money. Often, the risk is negligible. But sometimes, it's pennywise and pound-foolish. For example, when you're negotiating a contract of strategic significance with a large public corporation, expert legal advice is highly advisable despite the extra cost. Just because I had attended law school – at Harvard, no less

– didn't mean that I knew what I was doing. In an effort to save $5,000, I had imperiled millions. I was the living embodiment of Abraham Lincoln's admonition: "He who represents himself has a fool for a client."[30]

HEY KOOL-AID!

After two years in the entrepreneurial wilderness, LiveCapital had, at long last, raised some money. A seed round of $560,000 had been followed less than a year later by a $3.1 million Series A. And now again, less than a year later, we were close to finalizing a $10.7 million Series B.

The stars had miraculously aligned. In May, NextCard – the first credit card issuer to offer instant online approval – had gone public. Then in June, E-Loan – one of the first online mortgage lending providers – had followed suit. Now it was September, and we were on the verge of launching the first online marketplace for small business loans, a product that combined elements of both NextCard and E-Loan. Like NextCard, we would enable credit applications to be approved in real time. Like E-Loan, we would provide access to loans from many different lenders. Moreover, we had a significant first-mover advantage. We had spent more than a year building our platform – a flexible decision engine that enabled simultaneous, real-time underwriting across multiple financial institutions. We were the only company to have partnered with Fair Isaac (FICO), the world's leader in credit scoring. And we had convinced American Express to be the anchor tenant in our marketplace. The fact that many venture capital firms were interested in investing was hardly a surprise.

In the end, we decided to move forward with Kleiner Perkins. They had an excellent reputation, offered relatively attractive terms, and were locally headquartered in Silicon Valley, unlike Warburg Pincus, the other potential investor that we most actively considered. I also liked the partner from Kleiner Perkins who would soon be joining our board: Joe Lacob, future owner of the Golden State Warriors.

The progress we were making was undeniable, and the experience was exhilarating. After more than three years of adversity and struggle, everything, was somehow falling into place at exactly the same time. I remember feeling a surge of confidence in both myself and the company. We were going to succeed – in a very big way. I was certain of it. And more profoundly, we were going to change the world. Small business lending was only the beginning. Small business insurance was next. And beyond that? Only time would tell, but I was sure that the sky was the limit.

About two weeks before the round with Kleiner Perkins was scheduled to close, I received a voicemail from Doug Galen, VP of business development at E-Loan. In the message, he introduced himself and asked me to call him back as soon as possible. It wasn't hard to guess his motivation. E-Loan's stock price had soared since the company's recent IPO, and it now had a market cap exceeding $2 billion. As a result, they were well positioned to aggressively grow their business through strategic M&A. From an E-Loan perspective, LiveCapital was the perfect fit. E-Loan focused on consumer lending, while we were devoted to small business lending. Together, we would cover all the bases and become a dominant force.

When Doug and I spoke on the phone that afternoon, I enjoyed the conversation much more than I expected. We talked about the potential business synergies between E-Loan and LiveCapital, but a significant portion of the discussion focused on how well our values aligned. The call intrigued me enough that I agreed to meet in person at the E-Loan office in Pleasanton later in the week. Four people attended: me, my co-founder Scott Belser, Doug, and E-Loan's CEO (and future cryptocurrency multibillionaire) Chris Larsen – and we all immediately clicked. The meeting couldn't have gone better, and suddenly selling the company seemed like an option worth considering.

But we hadn't yet talked about price. That discussion came a week later at a ritzy hotel in San Francisco. Doug had decided to pull out all the stops. He arranged for the meeting to be held in a lavish penthouse suite, featuring a grand piano and stunning city views. This time, there were five people in attendance: me, Scott, Doug, Chris, and Joe Kennedy, E-Loan's new president and COO. After the requisite niceties, we got down to business, and Doug made the following pitch. He said that their offer was guided by the terms that Kleiner Perkins had recently provided to us. Since Kleiner Perkins had valued our company at $30 million, we were worth $30 million. Nonetheless, as "a reflection of their respect for us and commitment to our long-term mutual success," they were willing to pay a premium. His proposal, consequently, was for $40 million. Then he encouraged Scott and me to take as much time as we needed to consider our response, and he, Chris, and Joe retreated to the far side of the room.

Scott and I were disappointed. The offer of $40 million was less than 2 percent of E-Loan's market cap. And that didn't seem fair to us. Although their business was larger and farther along than ours, they had launched only two years earlier. Their technology platform wasn't as advanced as ours. They hadn't built a real-time decision engine because mortgage lending required numerous manual steps. Thus, even though the mortgage lending market was roughly 10 times larger than the small business lending market, it was harder to replicate what we had built. E-Loan was already facing significant competition, while we, at least for the moment, were the only game in town. We knew that we wouldn't have the market to ourselves for very long, but it seemed almost certain that our space would persistently remain less crowded. For all of these reasons, we believed that our relative value should be a lot higher than 2 percent.

That was the substantive discussion Scott and I quietly had while the E-Loan guys waited for our feedback. But there was also an emotional subtext. We were going to change the world, and we didn't need E-Loan to make that happen. We had Kleiner Perkins, American Express, and FICO in our corner. We had developed a technology platform unlike any that had been built before. Put it all together, and we had a huge competitive advantage. Why would we give all that up for less than 2 percent of E-Loan's value? The offer wasn't just low – it was insulting! Scott and I didn't talk about any of that, but it was implicit, at least in my head.

When we reconvened with Doug, Chris, and Joe a short time later, I provided our counteroffer: $200 million. No one spoke for a few seconds. Doug and Joe glanced over at Chris, who looked back at them, expressionless, as he contemplated what to say. Then he turned to look at me, and with the hint of a smile, softly observed, "Those numbers are very different." And with that, the meeting came to an end. The gap was too large. We parted on friendly terms, but the negotiation was over.

It was a monumental blunder on my part, and to this day – more than 25 years later – it remains my deepest professional regret. The memory is particularly painful because of how many unforced errors I made along the way. I should have told them that we needed more time to consider their offer, that we needed to speak to our board and investors, our other co-founder (my father), and the rest of the team. I should have gotten feedback from my wife. And Scott and I should have spent several days rather than several minutes reflecting and mulling over how best to respond.

But my most egregious mistake was losing sight of the bigger picture. At the time, my father and I still owned 50 percent of the company. We had raised only $3.7 million, so we hadn't been significantly diluted. If we had accepted E-Loan's $40 million offer, we would have received $20 million together. Furthermore, it's nearly certain that E-Loan would have agreed to a counteroffer of $50–60 million. At a $60 million price point, my dad and I would have received $30 million. That's a lot of money – way more than our family had ever possessed. My parents were financially secure, but hardly wealthy, and my wife and I, along with our then three-year-old son, had very limited savings. Moreover, Scott would have received $15 million, and the rest of the team would have also gotten a meaningful payout. A strong argument could have been made for declaring victory, selling the company, and then soon thereafter, starting a new company.

Unfortunately, I didn't consider any of these issues until after the moment had passed. When I counteroffered $200 million, I wasn't thinking about the impact the deal would have on my family or Scott or the rest of the team. Nor was I thinking about the many risks that our business still needed to overcome. I had completely lost perspective.

> **I had spent the past several months drinking my own Kool-Aid, and it tasted good. The problem wasn't greed, it was ambition – and ambition can sometimes be blind.**

Our company was acquired six years later. Neither my father, nor Scott, nor the other members of our original team, nor our original investors made any money. I made enough for a down payment on a house, but only about 5 percent of what I could have received from E-Loan.

I learned several important lessons. The first is that serious offers to buy your company are few and far between. When you get an offer, especially an offer where you and the other shareholders stand to make a lot of money, don't take it for granted. You might not get another offer like it. And second, when evaluating an offer to buy your company, take your goddamn time and don't let your emotions and ego get the better of you. Even if you ultimately decide to reject the offer, you'll have given it proper consideration.

LET THEM EAT STATIC

There is a moment that I particularly like in the film *Star Trek II: The Wrath of Khan*. Khan, a genetically engineered, megalomaniacal supervillain, has secretly hijacked the (starship) *Reliant* and is about to launch a vicious surprise attack on the *Enterprise*. Kirk, who is commanding the *Enterprise*, is oblivious to the danger. As the distance between the ships continues to narrow, he assumes that there must be an innocent explanation for the *Reliant*'s lack of response. Meanwhile, on the *Reliant*, the helmsman turns to Khan and says, "They're requesting communications, sir." With an arrogant smirk, Khan smugly replies, "Let them eat static." The attack commences shortly thereafter.

I can't say that I regard Khan as a kindred spirit. I've never been in combat, on Earth or in space, and I'm not homicidally inclined. Nonetheless, I've taken his words to heart. It's generally acknowledged that the "silent treatment" is a terrible way to build and manage relationships. But I've found that it can, on occasion, be a very effective negotiating technique.

All the companies I've sold have been acquired by other operating companies, with one exception. Zetta was acquired by Dover Equity Partners, an LA-based private equity firm. And the negotiating experience with Dover was very different – and much worse – than all the others.

Our strategic process got off to a conventional start. We retained a boutique, sell-side, investment bank – Architect Partners – created a pitch deck, organized a virtual data room, and created a list of potential acquirers.

Next, the Architect team reached out to the organizations we had identified, which led to a series of management meetings and, ultimately, a handful of bids. Dover was the high bidder.

Due diligence began within several days. The Dover team began examining the various documents in our data room to ensure they fully understood the nuances of our business and associated risks. As their review progressed, they periodically reached out to us with clarifying questions. In other words, everything was proceeding as usual. And then the principal from Dover, Matthew Henderson, gave me a call. He said that they had found something in their due diligence that had them concerned. Specifically, they didn't think our financial model's revenue-retention assumption was credible. As a result, he was compelled to reduce their bid.

This development was obviously unwelcome, but it wasn't catastrophic. The revised number was still meaningfully higher than the other bids we had received. Nonetheless, I wanted to better understand his rationale. The assumption questioned by Matthew and his team was based on historical performance. It hadn't been conjured out of thin air. So I asked him why he thought the assumption was wrong. To my dismay, he didn't have an answer that made any sense. Oh, he spoke a lot. There was an avalanche of words. He expressed himself with confidence and conviction. But he offered no data to support what he was saying. And the more questions I asked, the more frustrated he became. I soon realized that the supposedly faulty assumption we had made was merely a pretext. He just wanted to reduce the price. I told him that I needed to think about it.

My first instinct was to react emotionally and reject what he was saying out of hand. Unfortunately, we didn't have any leverage. If I responded assertively, I might very well kill the deal, and where would that leave us? None of the other bids were financially appealing, and for various reasons, remaining independent wasn't a viable alternative. Accordingly, the following day, I called him back, took a deep breath, and accepted the revised amount.

Then, two weeks later, the situation repeated itself. Matthew called me again and provided another nonsensical pretext for further lowering the amount they were willing to pay. Once more, I felt like flipping him off. And once more, I grudgingly agreed in the end.

Two weeks later, he tried the same thing a third time. It was now abundantly clear to me that this was Matthew and Dover's playbook. They would initially bid high to maximize the chance of being selected, but with no intention of actually paying the price they had offered. Instead, they would wait until due diligence was underway and then start inventing reasons why the price needed to be reduced.

This time I decided enough was enough. Maybe Matthew would walk away if I refused to play ball, or maybe he was just playing me for a fool. I had no way of knowing. What I did know was that if I didn't make a stand, he would keep moving the goalposts. However, my instinct told me that if I directly confronted Matthew, he would respond with defensiveness and hostility, increasing the chance that the deal would spontaneously combust.

> **I chose instead to channel my inner Khan. I didn't contact Matthew for the next three days. On the fourth day, he reached out to me. I politely told him that my board wasn't willing to agree to his most recent offer, and that the price couldn't be lowered again if he wanted to do the deal. He quickly acquiesced.**

The truth was that he had been playing me for a fool, and successfully so. In addition, I had been wrong in thinking that I had no leverage. As ultimately became clear, he was eager to make the deal. Otherwise, he wouldn't have so readily backed down. In retrospect, I should have invoked Khan's wisdom earlier. Perhaps I wouldn't have been able to avoid the first price reduction, but I'll bet that the second reduction could have been effectively resisted. My mistake was feeling that I needed to respond. Radio silence would have been a better approach. It would have helped to reveal Matthew's actual perspective.

I applied this lesson when I was at Inflection, negotiating to be acquired by Checkr. On several occasions, my negotiating counterpart – Checkr's CFO, Naeem Ishaq – staked out an aggressive position. And in every instance, I decided to "let him eat static." It worked every time. What I came to realize early on in the negotiation was that Naeem felt considerable pressure to get the deal done. I have no idea whether that pressure came from his boss (Checkr's CEO), Checkr's board, or if it was self-generated. But regardless, it meant that I had significant leverage. Radio silence proved to be an effective way to periodically and selectively use that leverage.

There is an adage that says, "We have two ears and one mouth so that we can listen twice as much as we speak." I've found that in a negotiating context, especially a zero-sum negotiating context, sometimes it's best not to speak at all. I'm confident that Khan would agree.

EMBRACING YOUR INNER ZENO

I suppose I should be more grateful that most big companies suck. That they struggle to adapt and innovate. That they're so remarkably bureaucratic, risk-averse, and slow. That they're so easily outmaneuvered.

After all, if big companies were less deficient, Silicon Valley's thriving startup culture wouldn't exist, at least not in its current form. Imagine, for a moment, a world in which corporate behemoths were just as innovative, nimble, and bold as their smaller counterparts. In this alternative reality, most small companies would be unable to effectively compete. There would be relatively few entrepreneurs, relatively few startups, and relatively few, if any, venture capitalists. It's not, to my mind, an appealing scenario.

So, from one perspective, I'm happy that big companies have such severe limitations. But it's a double-edged sword. The reason is that, for better or worse, most small Silicon Valley companies need to work with big companies to succeed. And herein lies the problem. Whenever a small company does business with a big company, the big company sets the pace. Bureaucracy invariably triumphs over speed – 100 percent of the time, without exception. It's an immutable law of nature. The corollary is likewise immutable: The more strategic the proposed relationship, the slower things move. Again, 100 percent of the time, without exception. For an entrepreneurial CEO, there are few experiences more frustrating than dealing with a big company.

I was excited when Mastercard expressed interest in acquiring Tempo, as they saw what we were doing as highly strategic. Their global head of debit, Rick Lyons, understood that by leveraging our decoupled debit technology, Mastercard could significantly disrupt the US debit card industry and gain considerable market share at the expense of its archrival, Visa. My discussions with Rick had gone smoothly, and we appeared to be aligned on price.

The process, as explained to me by Rick, would start with some relatively rapid, high-level due diligence. Mastercard would make a formal information request. We would post documents to an online data room in response to that request. They would ask questions about some of the documents. We would provide answers to their questions. And then, a nonbinding term sheet would be negotiated. Rick thought it would take about six to eight weeks to complete all of these steps.

Once the term sheet was executed, a more intensive and time-consuming due diligence effort would immediately follow. Contract negotiation would come next, and then, ultimately, the deal would be consummated. According to Rick, the entire process – from start to finish – would take about six months. He apologized that Mastercard moved at such a glacial pace.

Thus began our descent into hell. As promised, Mastercard sent us a formal information request. But the request, instead of being "high-level," was exceptionally granular. Many of the documents they asked us to provide didn't yet exist, so we were forced to create them on the fly. It took us longer than I would have liked, about 10 days, to get everything back to them. Then we waited for several weeks and heard nothing. Eventually, I contacted Rick, who apologized for the delay and told me, "Not to worry. Everything is on track." About a week later, Mastercard sent us a long list of questions, along with a request for additional documents they hadn't originally asked for. This time it took us only three days to respond. And then, once again, we waited for several weeks, and nothing happened.

The framework was now in place. We would answer Mastercard's questions. Mastercard would go radio silent for several weeks. I would contact Rick, who would assure me that all was well. Then, a few days later, Mastercard would send new questions and ask for additional documents. And the cycle would repeat itself – over and over again. We would hurry. And then we would wait. And wait, and wait, and wait.

It took us more than four months, rather than six to eight weeks, to complete the "high-level" due diligence so that attention could finally shift to negotiating the term sheet. Within a couple of days, however, everything was put on hold. Mastercard had just hired a new CFO (Martina Hund-Mejean), and she didn't want any new strategic commitments made without her approval. A few weeks later, I was told that things were finally about to get unstuck, but that instead of scheduling a discussion, they wanted to send a written proposal. Two weeks after that, I received the proposal. It referenced a purchase price that was less than half of what Rick and I had originally discussed. Six months had now elapsed since Mastercard had initially expressed interest. And it was at this point that I realized the deal was doomed.

> **Every negotiation that I've ever had with a Fortune 500 company – and there have been many – has mirrored the same pattern. Everything takes a long time, and new obstacles are constantly introduced, even at the 11th hour, regardless of whether the deal ultimately comes together or falls apart. The same immutable laws always apply.**

When I was about 10, my father taught me about Zeno's paradox. The concept is that it's impossible to ever get anywhere. Let's assume that you're on a football field, on the 40-yard line, and want to score a touchdown. You start moving and go half the distance to the end zone. Now you're on the 20-yard line. So you go half the distance again. Now you're on the 10-yard line. So you go half the distance once more. Now you're on the 5-yard line. And so on. The point is that your destination is perpetually out of reach. You get closer and closer and closer to the end zone, but never succeed in crossing the goal line.

What my father didn't explain was that Zeno's paradox has a real-world application. That only occurred to me many years later when I began dealing with companies like Mastercard. It's a lesson that all small company CEOs need to eventually acknowledge and accept. If you want to do business with a big company, you'd better get ready to embrace your inner Zeno.

SELLING OUT

I had mixed emotions when Checkr acquired Inflection. From a financial standpoint, the deal was extremely appealing. The first time we considered selling the company, several years earlier, the highest bid we received was for less than $100 million. Then, when we decided to take the company public in Australia, it seemed for a brief moment that a $300 million valuation might be achievable. More recently, when we had looked into raising a round of growth capital, the proposed valuations ranged between $175 million and $200 million. Consequently, a $400 million transaction with Checkr far exceeded my expectations.

The problem with the deal had nothing to do with money. We had achieved an unambiguously good financial outcome for shareholders. Had we remained independent and not sold the company, it likely would have taken us an additional three to five years to achieve a comparable valuation. And that assumed things continued to go well, which was in no way guaranteed.

No, the problem had to do with our other two constituencies: employees and customers. From an employee standpoint, the deal was both a blessing and a curse. On the positive side of the ledger, every employee was making extra money because they were all shareholders. The amounts might not be life-changing, but they were meaningful, and that made people happy. In addition, they were all retaining their jobs. (Out of more than 300 people, there were only six exceptions, including me.)

That was the good news. On the flip side, Checkr didn't seem like a great place to work. I wasn't sure that my apprehension was justified, but I trusted my instincts. With only a few exceptions, none of the Checkr employees I had met seemed happy. While none of them actively complained to me about the company, neither did they express much enthusiasm. I found that surprising and worrisome, given how impressively their business was growing.

I also had misgivings about Checkr's CEO, Daniel Yanisse. Daniel was obviously very intelligent, but he didn't seem interested in learning anything about the people who were about to join his team. He never once asked me questions about people's personalities, work styles, professional goals, or interpersonal skills. Nor did he ever follow up when I offered, on several occasions, to talk with him about these topics.

Even in the best of circumstances, combining companies is a daunting challenge. However, it's especially difficult when the cultures are misaligned. Inflection was exceptionally devoted to its employees. This heartfelt commitment reflected the warmth, empathy, and authenticity of the company's founders, Brian and Matthew Monahan. Unsurprisingly, employee satisfaction was always remarkably high. I doubted that the same could be said for Checkr.

I also had concerns about what Inflection's customers were about to experience. While Checkr generated most of its revenue from large gig-economy companies like Uber, Lyft, and DoorDash, our business was devoted to small- and medium-sized businesses (SMBs). We were both background-checking providers, but served very different customer segments. Inflection's rapid growth derived from our superior technology platform, product functionality, and customer support model – all tailored to meet the needs of SMBs.

To some degree, Daniel regarded our SMB-related expertise as valuable. It was one of the main strategic justifications for the deal. But counterintuitively, he wasn't interested in maintaining our technology platform, product functionality, or customer support model. With respect to our technology platform, Daniel's opinion was rigid and nonnegotiable. He emphatically believed that it should be shut down. He had a strong philosophical conviction that a merger of Silicon Valley companies could not be successfully executed if their technology platforms were, in any way, combined. In other words, one of the platforms needed to be completely eliminated. That perspective didn't make any sense to me or our CTO, Siddharth Ram, but Daniel's decision was final. The consequence was that post-acquisition, our customers would be adversely affected. Inflection's product (GoodHire) would be replaced with an ostensibly "equivalent" Checkr product that was, in fact, objectively inferior. Key SMB-focused features would be lost, and our SMB-focused user experience – something we had rigorously refined over many years – would degrade, at least for a time. Moreover, our quality of customer support would diminish since Checkr planned to move away from the personalized, high-touch model that we had long employed.

All of this called into question why Checkr was willing to pay $400 million to buy us. Daniel had highlighted three key objectives: accelerating Checkr's progress in the SMB segment, increasing Checkr's revenue, and growing Checkr's team. But there was a fourth objective that he hadn't mentioned: eliminating us as a competitor.

Before Checkr and Inflection, background checking was a manual, highly commoditized process. Technology played a relatively minor role, even for the largest companies in the space: First Advantage, Sterling, and HireRight. Then the landscape shifted. The rise of the internet created a foundation for technological disruption. It became possible to automate many parts of the background-checking process that previously required human involvement. Checkr and Inflection were the two startups that had recognized and seized this opportunity. Although the companies targeted different market segments, both had leveraged modern technology to fundamentally improve the customer experience. We had both succeeded in delivering considerable customer value: faster turnaround, improved efficiency, greater accuracy, and stronger compliance – all at a lower cost.

Checkr was the larger of the two companies. Their decision to focus on gig-economy customers had enabled them to scale exceptionally fast. In their short, seven-year existence, they had increased revenue from nothing to nearly $500 million and achieved a valuation of $5 billion. Assuming they maintained their rate of growth, they would be the world's leading background-checking provider within the next few years. However, growth was starting to diminish. If they hoped to rapidly overtake their largest competitors, they needed to diversify their customer base. And they concluded that their best new opportunity was with SMBs. But Inflection stood in the way.

I had little doubt that Checkr would figure out, over time, how to effectively compete in the SMB segment. If they wanted to maximize their growth, however, they needed to remove Inflection from the equation. The implication was clear: Our competitive elimination was actually one of Daniel's main motivations for the deal, and it explained why he was willing to pay such a substantial premium. It also explained why he wasn't more curious about Inflection's team – and why he was relatively indifferent to the customer impact of discarding our product, platform, and support model.

Selling a company is an emotional experience. It's the culmination of many years of dedication, perseverance, and collective struggle. It's an acknowledgement – and a validation – of the extraordinary effort that you and your team have made. And it's a significant achievement. But when the deal is closed and the acquirer has taken control, the prevailing emotion for a CEO is an acute sense of loss.

I'm reminded of Brad Pitt's quote from *The Curious Case of Benjamin Button*: "I was thinking how nothing lasts, and what a shame that is."[31]

> **When your company gets acquired, it's not just an outcome; it's an ending. A chapter is forever closed, and everything that you and your colleagues worked so diligently to create – at every level of abstraction – will now inevitably change.**

Every aspect of the business system will be revised. The team will be reorganized. The culture will be supplanted. Whatever isn't destroyed will be assimilated. And resistance is futile.

The money, to be sure, provides a measure of consolation. As a CEO, the financial benefit you derive is often significant. But it comes at a cost, especially if your heart is in the right place. When you sell a company, it's not just about you. And it's not just about shareholder return. There are other considerations. Your employees and customers also matter – a lot. So when fiduciary duty compels you to make decisions against their interests, which is exactly what I thought happened when Inflection was acquired by Checkr, it doesn't feel great. You feel like you aren't merely selling your company; you're selling a part of your soul. In certain respects, you're selling out.

I HAVE MET THE ENEMY, AND IT IS US

I remember thinking: *It was nice while it lasted.* In the 11 months since introducing the world's first online marketplace for small business loans, LiveCapital had faced no direct competition. Banks, of course, continued to originate small business loans offline. But none had fully embraced the internet, and so there was no other website where a small business owner could apply for financing and get instantly approved. In addition, no other technology company had yet attempted to replicate our multibank approach.

The launch of PrimeStreet – the world's second online marketplace for small business loans – came as a shock. Kevin Talbot, PrimeStreet's founder, had spent the previous two years working as a venture capitalist at the Royal Bank of Canada (RBC). In recent months, he and I had spoken several times about the possibility of RBC investing in LiveCapital. I had assumed that his interest was genuine and had, consequently, shared many confidential details about our business, never once suspecting that Kevin had a hidden agenda.

I was outraged, but also concerned. PrimeStreet seemed a formidable threat. They had already raised $40 million, and their lead investor, RBC, had virtually unlimited resources. Their CEO, my good buddy Kevin, was a highly intelligent, ruthlessly ambitious guy, with detailed knowledge about our strategy and plans. Moreover, he and his team seemed remarkably adept – and better than us – at generating publicity.

In the months that followed, I spent an enormous amount of time and energy obsessing about PrimeStreet. At my behest, carefully monitoring PrimeStreet became one of our key activities. We closely scrutinized everything about their business that was publicly available, from media coverage to product functionality to messaging to bank relationships. I even tried to get access to private information by recruiting away PrimeStreet's VP of marketing, a decision that, in retrospect, was ethically indefensible. We also substantially increased our online advertising budget once we realized how much money PrimeStreet was spending.

From one perspective, our competitive rivalry with PrimeStreet was arguably beneficial because it helped me rally the organization. Having an enemy can be highly motivating. People work harder when they feel like they're engaged in mortal combat. And it was easy for me to frame the rivalry with PrimeStreet as a battle between good and evil given the history with Kevin.

However, the animosity I expressed toward PrimeStreet and Kevin wasn't simply a stage act. It was the way I truly felt. *Godfather* wisdom notwithstanding, the conflict transcended business and was highly personal. Consequently, my revised goal had two parts: I wanted to build a massive, transformative company and cause PrimeStreet as much pain as possible. My main objective, of course, was our own success. But I also hoped that PrimeStreet, and Kevin in particular, would fail in a dramatic and humiliating fashion.

Lo and behold, to my total astonishment, that's exactly what happened. My wish was miraculously fulfilled. Only 15 months after bursting onto the scene, PrimeStreet abruptly shut down. We once again had the market all to ourselves.

Initially, I was thrilled to hear the news. Within a few days, however, my perspective began to shift. The truth, upon reflection, was that PrimeStreet's demise was a disturbing development that heightened my concern about our own viability. Yes, we were clearly better run than PrimeStreet, but so what?

The more critical question was whether, given the market dynamics of the time, any small business lending marketplace could meaningfully succeed. And I was increasingly suspicious that the answer was no.

I eventually realized that my preoccupation with PrimeStreet had been a significant error in judgment. First, in response to their aggressive marketing campaign, I had foolishly increased our marketing investment by $3 million. That money was effectively flushed down the toilet because it produced practically no additional revenue. Stupid is as stupid does. More broadly, my hypercompetitiveness had led the company to divert its focus away from the priorities that were most important. Our core objectives – delighting customers and improving our economic performance – had nothing to do with competition. These were the topics that demanded our full attention.

> **I learned a fundamental lesson. While it's important to be mindful of competition, you need to run your own race. The odds of success are considerably greater if you resist being distracted by competitive noise.**

Through the years, I've had the chance to apply this lesson on multiple occasions. There is almost always an archnemesis that casts a giant shadow. At Inflection, it was Checkr. At SugarSync, it was Dropbox. At Tempo, it was Capital One. Sometimes your company is in a relatively strong position. Sometimes you're in a relatively weak position. Either way, the lesson is the same. You need to focus on your business. And you need to make sure that your team is focused as well.

All of the companies I've run have struggled mightily at one point or another. But competitive activity has never been the primary cause. Our problems have instead been either market-related, in which case a pivot has been required, or self-inflicted. In other words, we've always controlled our own destiny. Thus, the enemy that matters most isn't competition; it's underperformance.

WHAT THE HELL IS GOING ON?

"You won't understand what's going on in your company if you only ask the people who directly report to you." It was one of the most important pearls of wisdom that Bill Campbell ever shared with me.

I first encountered this challenge around the time that LiveCapital hired its 40th employee. I had installed a new head of operations who proved to be remarkably responsive. Whenever I made a suggestion or request, he and his team would quickly mobilize and take immediate action. It was very impressive, or so I initially thought. The truth, however, was that it was largely a mirage. What was actually happening was that whenever I suggested or requested something, the head of ops made it his top priority. He would then instruct his team to abruptly shift their focus. The result was destructive. People were increasingly frustrated, and many critical projects – especially those that required multiple weeks or months of sustained effort – were getting delayed.

I had a similar experience, some months later, with our new VP of engineering. Based on our daily discussions, I assumed for a while that everything was going fairly smoothly. But I had been oblivious to the bigger picture. In reality, relationships within the engineering team had become strained and contentious. Two camps had rapidly formed – engineers the VP had recently recruited and engineers who had joined the company prior to his arrival – and they were culturally incompatible. Moreover, the engineers with longer tenure didn't trust the VP and questioned his technical judgment. And there was increasing friction between engineering and other departments.

When I asked for Bill's advice, I thought he would focus on the tactical question of how best to restore team alignment and cohesion. Instead, he was more interested in discussing the overarching strategic question: How had I allowed dysfunction to fester in the first place? Bill explained that my approach had been based on two assumptions that were both fundamentally flawed. The first was that my direct reports would share everything I needed to know with me. And the second was that it would be inappropriate for me to bypass the chain of command.

I ultimately realized that there are many reasons you can't rely on direct reports for complete and accurate information. In the worst case, they're politically motivated. They care more about how they're perceived than how well the company performs, and consequently, hide information that might make them look bad. If you've made the mistake of hiring an executive like this, you need to get them out of the organization as quickly as possible.

But there isn't always a Machiavellian motive. In fact, there usually isn't. Sometimes an issue isn't disclosed because the person reporting to you doesn't think that the issue is important. Or they regard the issue as important but assume it's below your pay grade. Or they're busy and forget to mention the issue. Or most frequently, they don't even realize the issue exists, either because they're not paying close enough attention or one of *their* direct reports isn't sharing what they know.

As I learned from Bill, the solution is building strong relationships with folks across the company – in every department and at every level of the organization. Such relationships demand a significant time investment and a genuine commitment to helping people achieve their professional goals. To be clear, your objective should be to create a coaching tree rather than a network of spies. But in the process, you'll end up much better informed.

Ignorance isn't bliss, especially as a CEO. If you want to succeed, you need to know what the hell is going on. And that requires an ongoing effort to communicate with your entire team, not just your management team.

NEVER GIVE UP, NEVER SURRENDER

You've toiled away more than 60 hours a week, every week, for years on end, without interruption. You can't remember the last time you fully disconnected, even when you've been on vacation. You're out of shape, chronically sleep-deprived, and persistently stressed out. Your relationships with both family and friends have suffered, and they continue to suffer. Moreover, the company is struggling to hit its plan. Revenue growth, which for a while appeared to be accelerating, has recently slowed. You've tested several new ideas to regain momentum, but none of them have worked. There is still some money in the bank, but the amount is steadily diminishing because the company still isn't profitable. Your investors are passively supportive, but can't or won't do much to help. They either aren't willing or aren't able to provide much additional funding. As a result, you'll need to find a new lead investor soon. You've been down this difficult road twice before, needing to raise capital with the Sword of Damocles hanging over your head. On both occasions, you narrowly averted catastrophe. But whether this pattern will continue is entirely unclear. If you've learned anything, it's that survival is never assured.

> **You lean back in your chair, take a deep breath, close your eyes, shake your head, and ask yourself: "Why**

the hell am I doing this?" And then you open your eyes, lean forward, and get back to work.

I'm reminded of a scene near the end of one of my favorite films, *The Lord of the Rings: The Two Towers*. The situation is bleak and seemingly hopeless. Our heroes sit amid the devastation, drained and demoralized, their quest teetering on the edge of disaster. Nonetheless, Sam remains steadfast. He struggles to his feet, stares off into the distance, and tearfully yet resolutely declares, "It's like in the great stories, Mr. Frodo. The ones that really mattered . . . Folk in those stories had lots of chances of turning back, only they didn't. They kept going."[32]

I suspect that many CEOs frequently fantasize about giving up and leaving. Certainly, I have. In fact, on multiple occasions, giving up has seemed to me like the most sensible course of action. Nonetheless, I've consistently resisted the temptation and persevered.[33] I think that's almost always the best approach.

There are four key reasons, three of which are admittedly driven by emotion. First, if you're running a company, you're probably a completionist at heart. You likely hate the idea of quitting anything, especially when you're in a position of responsibility. So if you walk away, there is a good chance that you'll later regret the decision.

Next, you desperately want to believe that all the time you've devoted and sacrifices you've made have been worthwhile. That requires you to keep moving forward. It's the "sunk cost fallacy" – the idea that you should keep making an effort because of the effort you've previously made, which is fundamentally irrational. But rational or not, it's the way you feel. And consequently, if you leave, you'll end up wishing you hadn't.

Furthermore, regardless of your emotional fatigue, you know that there's always a chance of turning things around. There are many examples of Silicon Valley companies that figured out a way to snatch victory from the jaws of defeat. If you leave, you forego that possibility. It's like in the classic scene in *Dumb and Dumber*, where Mary (played by Lauren Holly) tells Lloyd (played by Jim Carrey) that the odds of them ending up together are "not good . . . like one out of a million." Lloyd, undeterred, enthusiastically responds, "So you're telling me there's a chance!"[34] Hope springs eternal. And so you carry on.

The fourth and final reason is more practical. Your investors are counting on you to see things through. If you don't and walk away, they're far less likely to invest in you again or provide an enthusiastic reference down the road. How you handle adversity in the short term, thus, can affect your opportunities in the long term. It's just a fact – having a reputation for reliability and grit is professionally beneficial.

When you've been beating your head for years against the entrepreneurial wall, there are plenty of reasons to want to cut and run. Life is short. You're miserably unhappy. The opportunity cost is too high. But it's never that simple. For various reasons, both emotional and practical, you're past the point of no return. And you have a job to do.

NO REGRETS

My father has observed that no matter how old we get, we never stop asking ourselves the question: "What do you want to be when you grow up?"

When I was eight, I wanted to be a pitcher for the New York Mets like my favorite player, Tom Seaver. At 10, I hoped to be a medical doctor until, on a cross-country trip with my parents and sister, I had the opportunity to visit the Mayo Clinic in Rochester, Minnesota, and was astonished to realize that hospitals are full of sick people. At 12, I planned to pursue a career in politics. By 15, however, having repeatedly lost elections for student government, I concluded otherwise. Then at 17, I decided I wanted to become a serial entrepreneur even though I barely understood the meaning of the term. But naively, I only thought in terms of starting businesses. I never thought about actually running them.

The truth is that I never aspired to be a Silicon Valley CEO. That emerged organically. In the words of John Lennon, "Life is what happens when you're busy making other plans."[35]

Despite the title of this chapter, I have a long list of professional regrets. Some relate to mistakes I've made. And there have been many. Others relate to events beyond my control. And there have been many of those as well. But I have no regrets when it comes to my choice of career.

Being a Silicon Valley CEO is a crazy career path, with endless practical and emotional peaks and valleys. It's a hamster wheel of continuous stress, turbulence, and unpredictability – and is most definitely not for everyone.

I recall, with great affection, how my cousin Cindy playfully teased me when she learned that I had quit my job and co-founded LiveCapital with my wife nine months pregnant. Cindy kidded, "What are you? A lunatic?!" I don't remember how I responded. I probably just laughed. With the benefit of hindsight, however, I know now that the answer is yes – not just because of the timing of my decision, but because of the path I had chosen to take.

> **Running companies in Silicon Valley really does require a certain level of lunacy.**

Nonetheless, in the words of baseball immortal Yogi Berra: "If I had to do it all over again, I would do it all over again."[36] In fact, looking forward, I'm inclined to give it another shot. I've run six companies. So why not seven?

What do I want to be when I grow up? I want to be a Silicon Valley CEO.

ACKNOWLEDGMENTS

I never intended to write a book. As I observed in the chapter "Feeling Lucky?," sometimes things just happen. In this case, three friends (all former colleagues) – Jared Waterman, Joe Nagy, and Peter Chantel – provided the spark.

It all started about two years ago while catching up with Jared via Zoom. I don't specifically remember what we were discussing, but it pertained to my experience as a CEO. I was in a philosophical mood that day and shared some reflections about the key lessons I've learned through the years. After politely listening to me pontificate for a while, Jared suggested that I write a book. I didn't initially take the suggestion seriously. But about two hours later, while having lunch with Joe, I mentioned what Jared had said, and Joe enthusiastically agreed. Then, during a phone call with Peter the following week, he had an exuberantly positive reaction when I told him what both Jared and Joe had said. And at that moment I decided – why not? That set things in motion.

I'm glad to have written this book, although I can't say that I enjoyed the writing process. Some days were particularly painful. I would stare at the screen for 20 minutes, finally write a sentence, immediately delete the sentence, stare at the screen for another 10 minutes, write a few words, rewrite the words, delete the words, stand up, walk around the house, sit back down, stare at the screen some more, check my email, and so on in a seemingly endless loop. There were many times, especially during the first couple of months, when I came close to walking away from the project. But as I mentioned in the chapter "Never Give Up, Never Surrender," I hate the idea of quitting anything, so I persevered.

My resolve was strengthened by the example set by my wife (Wati), my adult kids (Alex and Talia), and my parents (Marilyn and Dave). They are all very different people, but the common theme is that they don't rest on their laurels. They're always in the mode of invention and reinvention.

When I met Wati, she was a lawyer. Then she became a fashion designer and worked for some of the world's largest apparel brands. Then she started her own fashion line. Then she did a 180 and started a (remarkably interesting and important) magazine focused on fashion sustainability. She is perpetually in motion, constantly challenging herself to do things she has never previously done.

Alex spent four years in the film industry, traveling around the world as director Ron Howard's on-set assistant. Then he decided to take a chance, start all over, and pursue a career as a basketball coach.

Talia, who recently graduated from university with a degree in fine arts, is relentlessly creative. Her work is always unique and never generic. Moreover, she never takes shortcuts or compromises her artistic integrity.

Marilyn fashioned an entirely new career for herself as an art curator after the age of 50. She ultimately spent more than 15 years organizing a fascinating and diverse array of art exhibitions at Stanford University.

Meanwhile, Dave is the most proactively innovative person I've ever met. In his "retirement," he has contributed to multiple academic papers, filed multiple patent applications, written multiple poems and a song, and created a spark chamber ("a device used in particle physics for detecting electrically charged particles"[37]) as a museum exhibit for the Chabot Space & Science Center in Oakland, California.

Given that context, writing a book seemed less daunting to me than might otherwise be the case. Whenever writer's constipation hit, which happened to me on a nearly daily basis, I thought about my family's creative grit and got back to work.

My approach to writing this book was partly inspired by another family member. My sister, Elissa, is a professor of entrepreneurship at the University of Southern California and an excellent teacher. One of the things that makes her so good is that her approach is based on storytelling. When she was little, she was a fan of the *Choose Your Own Adventure* book series, where the reader makes choices that determine the plot. As an educator, she often applies a similar framework to the way she talks about entrepreneurship. The entrepreneur is on an adventure, and every time there is an important decision to be made, they get to choose which path the story will take. I tried to keep this sensibility in mind as I wrote.

Last but not least, I want to express my gratitude to one of our amazing cats: Mister E. Every morning, whenever I would start writing, he would eagerly hop up on the desk next to my laptop, lie down, stretch, and promptly fall asleep. He was always a reassuring presence, especially on the days when writer's block was driving me particularly crazy.

ABOUT THE AUTHOR

Mike Grossman has spent more than 30 years in Silicon Valley as an executive and entrepreneur. He has been CEO of a diverse array of innovative, VC-funded software companies (Inflection, LiveCapital, Tempo, Attributor, SugarSync, and Zetta), all of which were ultimately acquired. His experience also includes leadership positions at Intuit and Johnson & Johnson and board roles at a variety of companies, including Quicken and Borders. Mike started his career as a management consultant for McKinsey & Company in San Francisco and Sydney.

In addition, Mike holds an AB in economics and a JD from Harvard University. He is passionate about his family, his cats (four at present), international travel, science fiction films, tennis, basketball, and creative writing (when time permits). This is his first book.

ENDNOTES

1 Eve, Holly. "Venture Capital Is Not the Funding Reality of Most Startups—Here's What Is." *Forbes*, July 6, 2020, https://www.forbes.com/sites/hollyeve/2020/07/06/venture-capital-is-not-the-funding-reality-of-most-startups-heres-what-is/.

2 "Startup Statistics for 2026: A Comprehensive Analysis." Revenue Memo, February 4, 2026, https://www.revenuememo.com/p/startup-statistics.

3 Ghosh, Shikhar. "Why Most Venture-Backed Companies Fail." Harvard Business School, December 10, 2012. https://www.hbs.edu/news/Pages/item.aspx?num=214.

4 "*Apollo 13* Quotes." IMDb, accessed February 10, 2026, https://www.imdb.com/title/tt0112384/quotes/?item=qt1376837.

5 "Bret Harte Quotes." Goodreads, access February 10, 2026, https://www.goodreads.com/quotes/115191-the-only-sure-thing-about-luck-is-that-it-will.

6 "Prisoner, The (1967–68)." Screenonline, accessed February 10, 2026, http://www.screenonline.org.uk/tv/id/478691/index.html.

7 "*The Godfather* Quotes." IMDb, accessed February 10, 2026, https://www.imdb.com/title/tt0068646/quotes/?item=qt0361843.

8 Ibid.

9 Hayes, Adam. "Black Swan in the Stock Market: What Is It, with Examples and History." Investopedia, May 31, 2024, https://www.investopedia.com/terms/b/blackswan.asp.

10 Peters, Thomas J. "A Necessary Revolution in American Management: People, People, People." In *Selections from the Second National Labor-Management Conference*, edited by Peter L. Regner. (US Department of Labor, 1985).

11 "Spectre—Memorable Quotes." MI6, accessed April 1, 2026, https://www.mi6-hq.com/sections/movies/spectre_quotes.

12 Gilligan's Island. "Voodoo Something to Me," YouTube, 25:29, October 10, 1964, https://www.youtube.com/watch?v=8o00ELObDis.

13 "Dwight David Eisenhower Quotes." Goodreads, accessed February 10, 2026, https://www.goodreads.com/quotes/4083-in-preparing-for-battle-i-have-always-found-that-plans.

14 "Mike Tyson Quotes." Goodreads, accessed February 10, 2026, https://www.goodreads.com/quotes/7906324-everyone-has-a-plan-until-they-get-punched-in-the.

15 "Eleanor Roosevelt Quotes." Goodreads, accessed February 10, 2026, https://www.goodreads.com/quotes/319111-it-takes-as-much-energy-to-wish-as-it-does.

16 "*Wall Street*, Charlie Sheen: Bud Fox." IMDb, accessed February 10, 2026, https://www.imdb.com/title/tt0094291/characters/nm0000221/.

17 "Larry Bird Quotes." AZ Quotes, accessed February 10, 2026, https://www.azquotes.com/quote/990197.

18 Mariah Carey. "Mariah Carey—Hero (Official Lyric Video)." YouTube, 4:18, September 8, 2023, https://www.youtube.com/watch?v=fDb0tKHcZhg.

19 StillWatchingNetflix. "Will Buxton Kinda Ate with the Spoon Analogy." YouTube, February 26, 2024, https://www.youtube.com/shorts/K_bxlTCO__8.

20 "No. 5: Chorus & Solo (Ko-Ko) 'Behold the Lord High Executioner.'" The Mikado, accessed February 10, 2026, https://www.gsarchive.net/mikado/webopera/mk105.html.

21 "*The Godfather Part II*, Lee Strasberg: Hyman Roth." IMDb, accessed February 10, 2026, https://www.imdb.com/title/tt0071562/characters/nm0833448/.

22 "*The Office* Stress Relief Quotes." IMDb, accessed February 10, 2026, https://www.imdb.com/title/tt1248736/quotes/?item=qt5749924.

23 Eliot, T. S. "The Hollow Men." Poets.org, accessed February 10, 2026, https://poets.org/poem/hollow-men.

24 Joel, Billy. "Honesty." Genius, accessed February 10, 2026, https://genius.com/Billy-joel-honesty-lyrics.

25 "I Have Good News and Bad News." *Bloomsbury Academic* (blog), March 6, 2019,

https://bloomsburyliterarystudiesblog.com/2019/03/i-have-good-news-and-bad-news.html.

26 "Garrison Keillor Quotes." Goodreads, accessed February 10, 2026, https://www.goodreads.com/quotes/64613-that-s-the-news-from-lake-woebegon-where-all-the-women.

27 Nunnally, Taylor. "Best Quotes from *Talladega Nights*: The Ballad of Ricky Bobby." Nascar, October 19, 2016, https://www.nascar.com/gallery/best-quotes-from-talladega-nights-the-ballad-of-ricky-bobby/.

28 "*Borat* Quotes." IMDb, accessed February 10, 2026, https://www.imdb.com/title/tt0443453/quotes/.

29 Cher. "If I Could Turn Back Time." Genius, accessed February 10, 2026, https://genius.com/Cher-if-i-could-turn-back-time-lyrics.

30 "Quote Origin: A Man Who Is His Own Lawyer Has a Fool for a Client." Quote Investigator, July 30, 2019, https://quoteinvestigator.com/2019/07/30/lawyer/.

31 "*The Curious Case of Benjamin Button* Quotes." IMDb, accessed February 10, 2026, https://www.imdb.com/title/tt0421715/quotes/.

32 "J.R.R. Tolkien Quotes." Goodreads, accessed February 10, 2026, https://www.goodreads.com/quotes/7444411-it-s-like-in-the-great-stories-mr-frodo-the-ones.

33 On one occasion, I stepped aside as CEO and became the company's executive chairman.

34 "*Dumb and Dumber* Quotes." IMDb, accessed February 10, 2026, https://www.imdb.com/title/tt0109686/quotes/?item=qt0383426.

35 "John Lennon Quotes." Goodreads, accessed February 10, 2026, https://www.goodreads.com/quotes/12575126-life-is-what-happens-when-you-re-busy-making-other-plans.

36 "Yogi Berry Quotes." QuoteFancy, accessed February 10, 2026, https://quotefancy.com/quote/941732/Yogi-Berra-If-I-had-to-do-it-all-over-again-I-would-do-it-all-over-again.

37 Joo, Kyungkwang, et al. "Development of a Spark Chamber by Using a Thyratron." *Journal of the Korean Physical Society* 55(6), December 2009, https://www.researchgate.net/publication/239010299_Development_of_a_Spark_Chamber_by_Using_a_Thyratron.